D1142057

PARENTS' DUTIES, CHILDREN'S DEBTS

Parents' Duties, Children's Debts

The limits of policy intervention

edited by
HARTLEY DEAN

arena

Published by
Arena
Ashgate Publishing Limited
Gower House
Croft Road
Aldershot
Hants GU11 3HR
England

Ashgate Publishing Company
Old Post Road
Brookfield
Vermont 05036
USA

British Library Cataloguing in Publication Data

Parents' Duties, Children's Debts: Limits of Policy
Intervention
I. Dean, Hartley
362.82
ISBN 1 85742 298 8

Library of Congress Catalog Card Number: 95-77820

Printed and bound in Great Britain by
Hartnolls Limited, Bodmin, Cornwall

Contents

Acknowledgements

The editor is grateful to the University of Luton for allowing him time and facilities to undertake the compilation of this book and to Keir Gale for assistance with final preparations for publication.

Notes on contributors

David Barrett is Head of the Department of Professional Social Studies at the University of Luton. He comes from a social work background and has researched and written about children's and adult services in both the voluntary and statutory sectors. He is currently working on a cross-national comparison of juvenile prostitution.

David Berridge is Professor of Child and Family Welfare at the University of Luton. He is author/co-author of six books on services for children and families 'in need', the most recent being (with R. Sinclair and L. Garnett) *Social work and assessment with adolescents* (National Children's Bureau, 1995).

Richard Common lectures in public policy at Leeds Metropolitan University. He has written on community care, including (with N. Flynn) *Contracting for Care* (Joseph Rowntree Foundation, 1992), and has acted as a consultant to the Department of Health Social Services Inspectorate on community care implementation.

Hartley Dean is Reader in Social Policy at the University of Luton. He is author of several articles and books on welfare rights and social policy, including (with P.Taylor-Gooby) *Dependency culture: The explosion of a myth* (Harvester Wheatsheaf, 1992) and *Welfare, law and citizenship* (Harvester Wheatsheaf, forthcoming).

Kathryn Ellis is Lecturer in Social Policy at the University of Luton. She has researched and written about needs assessment for community care, including *Squaring the circle: User and carer participation in needs assessment* (Joseph Rowntree Foundation/ Community Care, 1993).

Rah Fitches is Senior Lecturer in Health Studies at the University of Luton. With a professional background in nursing, her academic interests are in Medical Anthropology. She has researched and written about health related issues amongst Asian communities in Britain, with special reference to children with learning disabilities.

Brynna Kroll is Senior Lecturer in Probation Studies at Brunel University College. She is co-author of *The Probation Handbook* (Longman, 1992) and *Probation Practice* (Longman/Pitman, 1995), and author of *Chasing rainbows: Children, divorce and loss* (Russell House, 1994).

Di Thompson is a Researcher at the University of Luton and is currently completing a doctoral thesis on *The social and political construction of 'care': Community care in the 1990s*. She has previously worked in community development and is involved with carers' groups.

1 Introduction: Family debts, biological liabilities

Hartley Dean

> The price of my privileges and prospects was paid by my parents' sacrifice. .... If it is a matter of debt, I have always been and shall ever be, an undischarged bankrupt. Fortunately, our relationships were rooted in beneficent self giving. There is no debt. They have bequeathed me an abiding sense of indebtedness, and I want to keep this.
>
> (Bowen Thomas 1968)

We none of us choose our biological parents. For most of us, however, it is possible to choose whether and when we have children. Are we therefore indebted to our parents for the gift of life or, having had no say in the decision which brought us into the world, do we owe them nothing? Conversely, do we owe an enduring responsibility for the children we may bring into the world or, to the extent that as independent social beings our children can never belong to us, is there a proper limit to our obligations?

It is difficult to think of more fundamental moral questions. None the less, beyond the academic spheres of theology and social anthropology, these are issues which are comparatively seldom subjected to systematic intellectual scrutiny. The ties of family and kinship, and of such associated calls as 'love' and 'duty', are complex and powerful influences in our lives. The impetus to debate them has tended of late to come from two very disparate quarters: first, the political New Right whose 'back to basics' moral crusade encompasses support for 'traditional' family values; secondly, feminists who have sought to confront the essentially gendered nature of family and kinship obligations.

This chapter sets out critically to examine aspects of these debates and to set the scene for the remainder of the book. The book's central preoccupation is with the role of social and public policy in defining and enforcing the mutual debts and liabilities of parents and children. The chapter will therefore start with a discussion of the extent to which such deeply personal matters can also be issues of political concern. We shall move on to discuss the sense in which 'the family' is itself a creature of ideology, to consider the significance of biology to the roles people fulfil within families, and to deal with questions concerning the perpetuation of human populations and the basis of human dependency. Finally, the chapter will outline the contents of the rest of this book.

Politics and the personal

While the slogan, 'the personal is political', is usually associated with feminist thinking (see, for example, Eisenstein 1984), the UK government's 'back to basics' slogan, signals the sense in which 'the personal' has indeed been politicised. 'Back to basics' was a rallying cry coined by Prime Minister John Major at the 1993 Conservative Party Conference, at which he enjoined his Party to 'lead the country back' not only to sound money and free trade, but also to respect for the family (*Guardian* 9.10.93). In the wake of a series of scandals surrounding the private lives of members of his government, Major was later to deny that his campaign had anything to do with personal morality, but many on the neo-conservative or 'Thatcherite' wing of the Party clearly thought otherwise. Ministers like Michael Portillo and John Redwood insisted in widely publicised speeches upon the need to promote 'traditional' values and 'loving' two parent families (*Guardian* 7.1.94). 'Back to basics' is redolent of the Thatcherite homilies of the 1980s concerning the value of 'family life' (see below). What is more, the slogan afforded an overarching theme to unify aspects of Conservative government policy. It justified for example the introduction of the Child Support Agency (see Chapter 2); the inclusion in the Department for Education's 'Parents Charter' of a list of parental responsibilities as well as rights; the announcement of new penalties exercisable against the parents of young offenders (see Chapter 4).

The precedent and intellectual underpinnings for this 'back to basics' approach to family policy appears to have come from the USA and what Roche (1992) defines as neo-conservative pro-familism. In a definitive statement, produced by a working seminar on family and welfare involving several leading American neo-conservatives, the family is eulogised as 'the main incubator of the habits of free citizens' (Novak *et al* 1987: xvi). This is the justification for a political defence of 'the family' as an institution and indeed for forms of policy intervention which 'must insist upon personal responsibility and social obligation' (*ibid*: 18). The thrust of policy specifically to emerge from such assumptions includes an emphasis on incentives for two parent families and family self-sufficiency, and increased obligations upon absent parents to make support payments for their children. However, Roche provides the following summary of the wider political objectives:

> Neo-conservatives see citizens' family duties as including those of husbands and wives, of parents and young children, and of mature children and old parents to respect and care for each other, ideally for life (1992: 115).

Neo-conservatives like Charles Murray (1984) are perhaps best known for their argument that it is the welfare state that is to blame for undermining family obligations and the 'civilising' influence supposedly associated with the acceptance of family responsibilities. However, on a visit to Britain, Murray emphasised that a neo-conservative policy approach should not therefore seek to excuse those who fail to observe their obligations as citizens:

> I want to reintroduce the notion of [personal] blame and sharply reduce our willingness to call people 'victims'. ..... It is impossible to tell someone persuasively that he did well regarding one form of behaviour unless he may also be told that he did badly regarding another. Blame is essential if one is to praise. (1990: 71-2)

Clearly, John Major's 'back to basics' is not so radical or overt in its desire to enforce the acceptance of family responsibilities, but the point to be drawn is that any form of family policy involves a politicisation of 'personal' responsibilities and a potential for coercive intervention.

Personal life and familial obligations have been politicised in a very different sense through the rise of feminism. The whole of our discussion so far has been conducted without reference to gender and to the difference in the experiences and significance of family and kinship for women as opposed to men. Pascall makes the point that the very term 'family' can so readily become 'a unit of analysis in which women's particular interests are often submerged' (1986: 4). For women, far more than for men, the debts and responsibilities of family and kinship are directly associated with 'caring'. In her study of people caring for elderly relatives, Clare Ungerson found

> there were variations between carers as to hierarchies of obligation, disagreements among them as to how far other, particularly their own children,

> should be similarly obligated, expectations among many of them that the nature of 'good' behaviour could and would alter over the generations, and an understanding that the quantity and quality of state intervention in provision for dependent people was a major determinant of the basis for private morality. (1987: 142).

Yet, in spite of such variations and differences, all these carers felt 'that gendered kinship formed the basis of a general system of morality' (*ibid.*). The duty to care, whether for children or for aged relatives falls primarily to women and reflects relations of power based on patriarchy (which may be defined as 'the power of adult males over women and children, particularly in the family' (Fox Harding 1991: 13)).

Familial obligations therefore lie at the heart of feminist politics, not in the sense that women are struggling merely to be relieved of such obligations, but in a sense which takes the analysis of power to the level of interpersonal relationships. This is most clearly expressed by Hilary Graham, who has sought to bridge the gap between explanations of the way in which women's identity as carers (for children and aged relatives) has been fashioned and explanations of the way in which women's labour (paid and unpaid) is exploited: 'caring defines *both* the identity *and* the activity of women in Western society. It defines what it feels like to be a woman in a male-dominated and capitalist social order' (1983: 30). From this perspective, matters of love and duty are more than just personal. Caring in families may be driven both by affection and obligation, but is often experienced 'as a labour of love in which the labour must continue even where the love falters' (*ibid*: 16). Policy interventions which aim to manipulate the nature of such caring therefore run the risk of generating divisions within families (Ungerson 1987) or of going counterproductively 'against the grain' of people's expectations of family relationships (Dean and Taylor-Gooby 1992).

One of the most important contributions to an understanding of family and kinship obligations has been made by Janet Finch (1989b). She argues that, while assistance from relatives is important to most people, there is considerable diversity in the ways in which this is in practice organised and negotiated. In general, in white Western society, the 'inner circle' of the immediate family is the most important potential source of such assistance, but to the extent that membership of such inner circles may overlap in complex ways, the 'gendered hierarchy' referred to by Ungerson does not operate on the basis of fixed rules. Finch underlines the ways in which the morality of interpersonal obligation is in fact negotiated in real time between real people. The evidence, from the days of the coercive Victorian Poor Law to the present, is that

> On each occasion when government was attempting to impose a version of family responsibilities which people regarded as unreasonable, many responded by developing avoidance strategies: moving to another household, losing touch with their relatives, cheating the system. If anything it has been the state's assuming responsibility for individuals - such as the granting of old age pensions - which has freed people to develop closer and more supportive relationships with their kin. It seems it is not in the power of governments straightforwardly to manipulate what we do for our relatives, let alone what we believe to be proper. (1989b: 243)

Personal questions relating to the care we give and receive in our families are therefore political, both in the narrow sense that there are politicians who seek to exercise influence over them, and in the broad sense that in daily life they are negotiated between people (men and women, parents and children, old and young) with differing degrees of power.

Ideologies of the family

Former Prime-Minister Margaret Thatcher once declared that 'it all really starts with the family .... its the place where each generation learns its responsibility to the rest of society' (1981). Ironically, however, she was later to make that now famous announcement that 'there is no such thing as society, only individuals and their families' (1988). These apparently contradictory statements in fact contain the essence of a coherent ideology based on antipathy to collectivised state provision and a reification of the self-sufficient family unit.

Diana Gittins, in contrast, has argued that 'there is no such thing as *the* family' (1993: 8). The point she makes is that while families are real, changing and diverse, the concept of the 'the family' is no more than an ideological construct. Gittins' is one of several critiques of functionalist accounts of the family as a secular institution.

Conventional historical and sociological accounts of the family have tended to assume that in preindustrial society families were more extended and mutually supportive, while the nuclear family - consisting of co-residing husband, wife and dependent children - is a relatively modern phenomenon. Whereas the pre-industrial family had important functions as a unit of economic production, the modern family is more 'specialised' in its role. Productive functions have been subsumed within the market economy and certain social reproductive functions relating to health, personal care and education have been transferred to the welfare state. The functions remaining to the family as an institution relate therefore to the primary socialisation of children and the maintenance of adult personalities (Parsons 1964). Such conventional wisdom has been applied on the one hand to valorise the 'modern' nuclear family and the intensely private space it occupies as the foundation of social stability and freedom in a complex industrial society (Berger and Berger 1983). On the other hand, such wisdom can also on occasions nourish expressions of regret for the passing of an imagined age in which families and communities exhibited more solidarity (see Lasch 1977; Mount 1982).

Affection for the ideal of the 'traditional family' is by no means the preserve of the political Right. A.H.Halsey, the distinguished academic and ethical socialist, has roundly blamed the 'cult of individualism' for what he sees as the current 'frailty' of the family as an institution. Margaret Thatcher, he suggests, 'may well be seen .... as a major architect of the demolition of the traditional family' (1993: 129). Declining fertility and the rising incidence of divorce and lone parenting in affluent Western countries represents, Halsey fears, a 'flight from parenthood' and a tendency for the economically rational, egotistical individual (and particularly men) to opt out of familial obligation. Recognising some of the imperfections of the institution, Halsey denies that there was a golden age of the family, but he none the less insists, in language remarkably reminiscent of Margaret Thatcher's, that there was a traditional family system prior to the 1960s which provided 'a coherent strategy for the ordering of relations in such a way as to equip children for their own eventual adult responsibilities' (*ibid.*)

Historical analyses, however, (Laslett 1972; Anderson 1971; Stone 1977) suggest a rather complex picture. Families in the pre-industrial era were often more nuclear in structure than extended, whereas the dislocations of industrialisation often generated rather than undermined patterns of extended kinship support. The dismantling of feudal social relations was reflected, less in changes in family structure, than in shifts in values. Allegiances to land, liege and lineage were displaced, initially in favour of subservience to state and church and, in particular, to the patriarchal family head. The subsequent ascendancy of capitalism and the ideology of bourgeois individualism were associated with notions which valued privacy and close emotional bonds as a basis for a different kind of family life. Real families have at all times remained diverse in form and structure and Gittins and others argue it is impossible to characterise any particular historical period with reference to any particular kind of family. What can none the less be identified historically is the emergence in the eighteenth and nineteenth centuries of that very particular familial ideology, associated originally with the new industrial middle-class, but which became increasingly universal as, for example, trade unions began to campaign for a 'family wage' sufficient to support a male worker and his dependent wife and children.

Since the nineteenth century socio-economic and demographic changes have transformed the circumstances in which families form or are dissolved and in which the realities of family life are lived out. Trends in fertility, mortality, household formation, social and geographical mobility, women's participation in the labour force, the incidence and acceptability of marriage, divorce, co-habitation, single parenthood and same-sex partnerships have all together resulted in a situation in which

> While everybody at some point will share space, time, skills, sexuality, affection and love with others, the ways in which individuals live, struggle and interact together are too varied to be able to encase these activities into a term such as 'the family'. (Gittins 1993: 167)

Real families do not always conform to any theoretical or ideologically determined model, but even if they do they can be dangerous places. Radical psychiatrists like Laing (1971) and Cooper (1972) have argued that the claustrophobic nature of the 'ideal' nuclear family damages rather than nurtures the human psyche. Feminists and other commentators point to the incidence in families of physical violence and sexual abuse against women, against children and against aged relatives. Although this book is primarily concerned with intergenerational obligations, dysfunctional relations between partners within families inevitably have an impact upon how and by whom obligations to children and/or elders may be discharged. Violence by men against female partners and inequalities in the distribution of income within partnerships (see Pahl 1985 and 1989) will often constitute a part of the context in which wider familial duties are constructed and understood.

In spite of this, the ideologies of 'the family' endure and obscure rather than illuminate questions of how our duties and obligations to children, parents and other relatives may be worked out in practice. To return to Janet Finch, she has pointed out how notions of family obligation which appeal to ideologically generated constructions of 'traditional values' may have little foundation in fact. In mediaeval times, for example, childhood as a stage of dependency upon parents would have ended at the age of seven (see Gittins 1993: 8). In the age of Victorian values, comparatively few people would have survived into frail old age and the obligation to care for elderly relatives was one which 'was simply not put to the test for most people in previous generations' (Finch 1989b: 81).

Biology and welfare

The obligations and duties which we are discussing arise in the context of relationships which are biologically determined as well as socially circumscribed. However, while human parents may share with animals forms of behaviour which are related to the protection and nurturing of immature offspring, human behaviour is generally accepted to be almost entirely acquired rather than innate (Broadhurst 1963). In terms of animal biology the 'pay off' which arises from 'successful' parenting behaviour is achieved unconsciously through the mechanism of natural selection and the survival of the species. A social Darwinist perspective might correspondingly suggest that effective parenting and its perpetuation from generation to generation will represent a necessary characteristic for the survival of a society. This view and, in particular the idea that good 'mothercraft' was an essential prerequisite for national efficiency, has at times been an important influence in the development of social policy (see, for example, Williams 1989). Such thinking, however, raises two important questions: first, what is the basis for human behaviour towards children or adults who by reason of infirmity, impairment or advanced age have no potential contribution to make to the survival of the species?; second, what is the basis in human societies for the particular sexual divisions of labour which have developed around parenting behaviour and caring for biological kin?

Anthropologists suggest that modern bureaucratically ordered societies no longer require the systems of kinship loyalty which had been necessary to more 'primitive' societies. Duties owed to aged relatives would once have been essential to the mechanisms by which power and property were regulated and passed between generations, but survive now as the 'accumulated, almost innate wisdom of the blood' (Fox 1967). Blood relationships undoubtedly remain socially important, but their practical maintenance is and has never been biologically necessary. Similarly, the strictly gendered roles of motherhood and fatherhood do not result from a biologically necessary division of labour. While a sexual division of labour between female nurturers and male providers may have emerged in certain hunting/gathering societies, the perpetuation of such divisions owes nothing to mechanisms essential for the reproduction of the species. Kathleen Gough (1975) has suggested that exploitation based, not only (as Marxists would argue) on class divisions, but also on gender would have sprung from the development of the capacity to produce an economic surplus and from the growth of the state: such developments gave rise to powerful roles for men outside the bounds of kinship groups and made it possible for women's roles to be defined in accordance with men's interests. The point therefore is that the significance of blood ties and gender roles alike is socially rather than biologically determined.

Dealing for a moment with the notion of blood ties, Lorraine Fox Harding has suggested that one way of thinking about the issue is 'to point out that families are socially defined, but that society defines them in biological terms' (1991: 118). She calls particular attention to the distinctions between psychological and biological parenthood (see Chapter 3 in this volume) and the debate between those who believe, on the one hand, that the quality of parental care is more important than the existence of a genetic relationship and those, on the other, who contend that biological ties matter because of the fundamental sense of identity which comes from knowing where one has 'come from' (which may be especially salient for people from ethnic minorities). The lengths to which adopted children sometimes go in adulthood to discover the identity of and to meet their 'natural' parents is testimony to the strength of this need for identity. Bob Holman (1988) makes the point that stigma can even attach to children not having natural parents, simply because such biological ties are socially constituted as a part of being 'normal'. Individual identity and social normality are therefore defined in a biological context.

Feminist psychologists (Chodorow 1978; Gilligan 1982 - discussed in Ungerson 1987) have further suggested that women's particular sense of identity is fashioned in the context of human relationships and in their capacity to care for dependants. For women and girls rather than for men and boys identity does not depend upon childhood separation from their mothers and the processes of individuation which follow. The moral strengths of women therefore lie in relationships and the exercise of responsibilities rather than, as for men, in independence and the exercise of rights. We have seen above that Hilary Graham believes that caring indeed defines the identity of women in Western society, but she also argues that it defines women's activity and the requirements which are placed on women. Caring is a product not only of symbolic bonds, it is also represents a political and economic relation. Identity and sense of familial duty is fashioned in the context of biological relationships and sexual differences, but Graham counsels against the dangers of essentialism and explicitly rejects the idea that the moral duty to care is simply a reflection of 'women's biological nature and women's psychic needs' (1983: 28).

It is important at this juncture to discuss differences within feminism about the nature of women's subordination and the significance this has for the biological context in which social obligations are constructed. In a seminal and wide-ranging analysis, Fiona Williams (1989) has distinguished and criticised several different strands of feminist analysis, looking amongst other things at the particular role that biology plays in such analyses. She is critical of what she calls *liberal* feminism, that strand of feminism which is primarily concerned with preventing discrimination and fostering formal equality, precisely because it neglects the significance of the biological dimension to women's role. *Libertarian* feminism's insistence that 'a woman's place is where she chooses to be', can result either in a similar denial of women's biology or else in an idealist reverence for motherhood and family. *Welfare* feminism and *radical* feminism, Williams accuses of being biologically determinist: welfare feminism embraces women's biology as their destiny and has campaigned, for example, for the endowment of motherhood through family allowances; radical feminism in contrast identifies patriarchy as the endemic cause of all women's oppression and would pursue resistance to patriarchy through the development of an exclusively 'women's culture' which elevates those values which women, 'by their nature', possess. Williams herself identifies more strongly with *socialist* feminism and *black* feminism because they each in differing ways embrace women's biology, while situating it in the specific social, historical and material conditions through which patriarchy and the processes of biological and social reproduction are constituted.

Population and humanity

Politics and ideology, gender and biology; all are implicated in the way that our duties to children and parents are constituted and experienced; and all are controversial, contested factors. Overarching such controversies are still more fundamental questions about why human populations should sustain themselves through mutual care and support. The population of Great Britain has increased from around 9 million in 1800 to around 55 million at present. US ecologist, Pimentel (1994), has estimated that, whereas the Earth as a whole is capable of indefinitely supporting a population of just 2 billion people, its present population stands at 5.6 billion, and at present rates of increase could reach 12 to 15 billion by the year 2100 - around seven times the level of global sustainability. The propensity of the human species, not only to multiply, but also in more technologically advanced societies 'unnaturally' to protect, nurture and extend the lives of its members may pose a threat to the survival of the species itself. These issues and their implications for everyday behaviour have lately been addressed by the green movement and, in the case of so called 'deep ecology', by way of draconian proposals which challenge the very basis of the morality on which people care for each other (Ferris 1991).

Such concerns, however, are not new. In the late eighteenth and early nineteenth centuries the now infamous Rev. Thomas Malthus (1798) was in fact only one of several proponents of the view that agriculture at that time could not support an accelerating population. According to Malthus, history proved that excessive increases in population must ultimately be curtailed by either famine, war or pestilence. Malthus' answer to the problem, which was reflected for example in aspects of the nineteenth century Poor Law, was to ensure through moral, if not coercive constraint that the poor should not increase in number. (The middle classes, it seems, were not thought to be in need of constraint.) Anti-populationist, even eugenicist, influences have been evident in the early development of state welfare - for example in the separation of the sexes in workhouses, mental asylums and colonies - and in subtle ways have left their mark on many of the more punitive aspects of the 'modern' welfare state (see Dean 1991).

Counterbalancing (but never eclipsing) these anti-populationist influences, have been more humanitarian, pro-populationist influences upon policy and personal behaviour. A century before Malthus, Lord Chief Justice Matthew Hale put it thus; 'the more populous the state or country is, the richer or more wealthy it is. But with us in England, for want of due regulation of things, the more populous we are, the poorer we are' (1683). This opposing strand of thought has at different times similarly left its mark in the development of social policy, not least in the development of family allowances (Land 1975) and other elements of policy by which society declares its stake in the well being of a future generation. A development of this pro-populationist perspective is to be found in human capital theory, an economic theory which espouses the view that 'the most valuable of all capital is that invested in human beings' (Marshall 1890). It is a theory which has more recently figured in elements of Labour Party policy (see Labour Party 1992), in the rhetoric of what has lately been dubbed 'supply side socialism' and the recommendations of the Commission on Social Justice (1994: ch. 7). Evidence for the beneficial effects of public investment in education, health and other services which enhance the quality of labour power is complex, but suggests on balance that social policy has been a positive force for economic prosperity (George and Wilding 1984).

The development of the welfare state has therefore reflected contradictory tendencies: on the one hand, policies which punish improvidence and overfecundity; on the other, policies which relieve people of the necessity to provide certain elements of care for their children and other dependants. Also reflected are different accounts of where moral duty lies: on the one hand, a view which holds us all accountable for our own dependants; on the other, a view that we are all dependants of society and it is the state which acts as guarantor of our collective responsibilities. The emphasis within social policy upon these competing interpretations shifts over time and, in Britain during the 1980s and '90s has shifted significantly in favour of the enforcement of individual rather than collective responsibilities to care. Attention in policy terms is directed to issues of dependency, rather than population. Ecological concerns about the limits to the human population's exploitation of natural resources remain unaddressed.

Dependency and exploitation

This book will argue that notions of dependency and exploitation are central to the analysis of familial obligation. Dependency and exploitation are intimately related. The human species' exploitation of the planet's natural resources is inseparable from the species' physical dependency on those resources. Class exploitation and, in particular, capital's exploitation of labour, arises because social existence is also dependent upon human labour power. Men's exploitation of women arises because of the interdependency that is required for the social reproduction of such labour power. Dependency in each instance is inevitable. Whether exploitation is the inevitable corollary of dependency is arguable.

The particular obligations which we are here discussing arise from the dependency of children and aged parents. Justification for those obligations may be expressed in terms of indebtedness and reciprocity; identity and attachment; custom and social practice; or policy and legal requirement. All these justifications are important to an understanding of the nature of familial obligations but they do not of themselves define the moral basis of the relationships in which obligations occur.

In different ways, sociologists from Durkheim to Marx have identified the sense in which, the more advanced societies are, the more inter-dependent its members become. However, the character of that inter-dependency is often obscured. This writer has argued elsewhere that, on both the left and the right of the political spectrum, there is a tendency to 'fetishize' dependency (Dean and Taylor-Gooby 1992: chs. 2 and 6). The classic Fabian justification for the welfare state was that the vicissitudes of the market generated unnatural 'states of dependency' which the state had a collective responsibility to ameliorate (Titmuss 1963). The right wing neo-conservative assault against that welfare state has been based on the denigration of the 'sullen apathy of dependence' and upon the assertion that human happiness and freedom is to be found through the quest for 'independence' (see Moore 1987). Neither of these views will embrace the reality that mutual dependency is a part of the human condition. Denying this reality conceals the extent of our dependency and therefore the relations of power upon which such dependency rests. Relationships of dependency are also relationships of power (see, for example, Walker 1982). Parents exercise power over children and carers exercise power over adult dependants. The dynamics of those relationships can be complex, however, and dependants themselves are not necessarily powerless. As Finch makes clear (see discussion above), power in relationships is a matter for negotiation based on the specific history and circumstances of each relationship. Additionally, parents and carers will themselves be enmeshed in relationships of dependency: they may to varying degrees be financially dependent upon another member of their family or upon state benefits; they may be dependent upon services and professional support. These relationships also involve elements of power. Parents and carers are seldom autonomous but are subject to control through the expectations of breadwinning spouses, the regulations of the social security system, the dictates of welfare workers and professionals.

The critical question for the contributors to this book is the point at which and the extent to which family debts and biological liabilities may be rendered exploitative. Not all debts and liabilities are burdensome as the quotation with which this chapter opens is intended to illustrate. However, our mutual dependency as human beings represents not only the fulcrum around which the definition of our humanity turns, it is also a point of leverage for the exercise of power over human behaviour.

Outline of the book

The contributions contained in this book are diverse in terms of their style and approach as well as their subject matter. They are bound together none the less by a focus upon the role of the state in regulating, prescribing or defining parent-offspring relations.

Chapters 2 to 4 are concerned with parents' responsibilities for young children. Chapter 2 discusses the controversies which have surrounded the 1991 Child Support Act and the issue of parents' liability to support financially their biological offspring. In Chapter 3 David Berridge discusses the concepts contained in the 1989 Children Act and, in particular, the way in which this legislation defines the mutual responsibilities of parents and the state when families are in crisis. These issues are taken further by Brynna Kroll and David Barrett who, in Chapter 4, discuss the role of the youth justice system and the ways in which the state articulates with parents and children when children prove 'troublesome'.

Chapter 5, by Rah Fitches, is a salutary reminder that the nature of parent-offspring relations is not universal, but culturally specific. The chapter raises fundamental issues about the proper limits of state intervention in child rearing practices.

Chapters 6 to 8 are concerned primarily with the responsibilities which adult children have for their elderly, frail or disabled parents. In Chapter 6 Kathryn Ellis discusses the introduction of the community care provisions of the 1990 NHS and Community Care Act and, in particular, the part the state now plays in defining the needs of parents in their later years and the duties of children to meet those needs. Di Thompson in Chapter 7 takes these issues further, examining the way in which the caring responsibilities of adult children - especially daughters - are being socially and politically reconstituted. In Chapter 8, writing from within a rather different tradition, Richard Common also discusses the 1990 NHS and Community Care Act, but taking as his theme the ways in which the state is involved in 'contracting out' the liabilities which children and parents may have for each other.

Finally, Chapter 9 attempts to draw together the themes which emerge from the book as a whole and will argue that, while the welfare state has an indispensible role to play in facilitating the 'beneficent self-giving' which so often characterises parent-offspring relations, it also exhibits a propensity for burdening such relations with debts and liabilities which are ideologicallly or historically fashioned, rather than merely biological in origin.

2 Paying for children:
Procreation and financial liability

Hartley Dean

One of the first duties which is universally assumed to fall upon parents is to 'provide' for their immature offspring. Providing may take many forms. In contemporary Western societies, when by choice or circumstance the parents of a dependent child may live separately, provision for the child's day to day care may be separated from provision for her/his financial support. In such circumstances, the state may step in to enforce the financial responsibilities of a non-custodial parent. This chapter will discuss Britain's child support scheme, as an instance of such intervention.

The scheme was introduced by the 1991 Child Support Act ('CSA') and came into force in April 1993. Though the changes brought about by the CSA were hailed as 'the most far reaching social reforms to be made for forty years' (SSC 1993: v), the Act's implementation has remained the source of curiously chaotic controversy. The assumption to which the scheme gives legal effect is that biological parents have an inviolable duty to support their children financially, regardless of any changes or breakdown in family or living arrangements. To enforce this duty the CSA provided

- a formula to determine the extent of an 'absent' parent's liability to maintain a dependent child with which he (or, less usually, she) does not co-reside, and
- an administrative agency (the Child Support Agency) with responsibility for assessing, collecting and enforcing child maintenance payments by absent parents.

The legislation, originally urged upon the government by a right-wing 'think tank', the Centre for Policy Studies, none the less received all-party support in the House of Commons. Social attitude data appears consistently to demonstrate that more than 90 per cent of the population accept that parents have a financial responsibility towards their children (Kiernan 1992; Taylor-Gooby 1994). In spite of this consensus at the level of political and public opinion, the introduction of the child support scheme generated unprecedented resentment and antagonism and there was a vociferous public campaign against the CSA. Offices of the Child Support Agency received hate mail containing razor blades, excrement and hypodermic syringes, and the home of the social security minister with responsibility for the Agency was daubed by protesters with graffiti (*Guardian* 22.3.94 and 6.4.94). Anger against the CSA was compounded by delays and inefficiencies on the part of the Child Support Agency, shortcomings which were admitted in the Agency's first full annual report (CSA 1994), and in September 1994 the first Chief Executive of the Agency resigned. A damning report by the Parliamentary Ombusdman subsequently found the Agency to have been guilty of maladministration during its first months of operation (*Guardian* 19.1.95).

The most strident opposition was orchestrated by irate (and largely middle-class) fathers complaining they had been unfairly targeted by the Agency. However, a different kind of protest was pursued by radical women's groups who complained that women were being coerced into reluctant dependency on men. Lone parent groups gave guarded support for the proposals (Slipman and Monk 1991). Some commentators endorsed the scheme as a way of 'imposing financial penalties on irresponsible penises' (Toynbee 1994). Others made predictions that it would do little or nothing to improve the lot of lone parents on low incomes and was likely to increase the extent of child poverty (Bennett and Chapman 1990; Millar 1993).

There have been considered assessments of the child support scheme (NACAB 1994; NCOPF 1994; Garnham and Knights 1994b; Clarke *et al* 1993 and 1994). These have concentrated in complex detail upon the operational failures of the scheme and have discussed how the principles of the scheme might better be put into practice. Additionally the House of Commons Social Security Select Committee has twice subjected the scheme to critical scrutiny (SSC 1993 and 1994), following which the government has on each occasion responded by making changes to the scheme. The most significant of these changes have still at the time of writing to be implemented. This chapter, however, will be concerned less with the details of the scheme than the underlying purposes to which it is directed. In what follows, I shall firstly outline the background to the legislation and the ideological aspirations of the scheme's supporters and opponents, before moving on to consider the implications of the legislation in practice.

Background to the Child Support Act

The CSA is a complex piece of legislation which is best understood in terms of its historical background and policy context, as well as in relation to the specific provisions which it contains.

Historical background

A general duty to support one's family, descendants or kin has been enforced since Tudor times. Under the Elizabethan Poor Law parish relief would be withheld from fatherless families if they had any living relative to whom they might otherwise turn for assistance. Single women who were pregnant had to name and either marry or exact maintenance from the putative father, but no specific mechanism existed to enforce such maintenance.

In the mid-nineteenth century it became possible in the secular Divorce Courts for affluent married women upon separation or divorce to obtain court orders against their husbands for periodical maintenance. Such remedies were not accessible to destitute single or deserted mothers. The Victorian Poor Law no longer required lone mothers to identify the fathers of their children, but the burden of moral opprobrium and rigours of the workhouse were calculated to encourage them to seek refuge elsewhere. When, in spite of this, the demands of deserted wives upon the Poor Law were thought to be rising unacceptably, the Matrimonial Causes Act of 1878 - in one sense, a precursor to the CSA - was introduced. This empowered Magistrates Courts to make separation and maintenance orders, including child maintenance orders, though only in favour of women whose husbands had been convicted of assaulting them (Hoggett and Pearl 1991).

The burden of maintaining children was becoming more onerous: factory legislation began to curtail children's hours of work and thereby their earning power; the introduction of compulsory education ensured that children remained dependent on their parents longer; and children therefore began to become a financial liability rather than an asset. By and large however, as Gittins puts it, 'so long as people did not become either a financial liability to the State or a threat to social and political order, despite the plethora of middle-class moralising, governments cared (and care) very little as to the actual living arrangements people entered to survive' (1993:142). This was to remain the case until the 1990s. The jurisdiction of both the Divorce Courts and the Magistrates Courts had continued to develop in relation to the making of maintenance orders for children following the separation or divorce of their parents or in affiliation proceedings brought against putative fathers. Prior to the divorce law reforms of the 1970s the Magistrates Courts' jurisdiction remained that which was routinely accessible to people of more limited means and differed in several respects from that of the Divorce Courts: unlike the latter, magistrates were subject to set limits with regard to the amount of child maintenance they could award.

The making of child maintenance orders depended upon the instigation of court proceedings by or on behalf of the parent/guardian with care of a dependent child and the amount of maintenance awarded, subject to the limitation mentioned, relied upon the courts' subjective interpretation of children's' needs and parents' respective circumstances. These were essentially private arrangements, in which the state's involvement was that of disinterested adjudicator.

Rather different considerations applied if the children concerned were members of a household in receipt of social assistance benefits. The 1948 National Assistance Act (and, in succession, the Supplementary Benefits Acts and 1986 Social Security Act) made all citizens statutorily liable to maintain their spouses and offspring. The legislation enforced the duty by empowering benefit administrators to seek voluntary agreements with or, failing this, to take court proceedings against, 'liable relatives' with a view to recovering the cost of social assistance benefits paid in respect of their children and/or separated (but not divorced) spouses. The vigour with which liable relatives were pursued tended to fluctuate depending on the prevailing priorities and exigencies of government policy (see, for example, Golding and Middleton 1982; Bradshaw and Millar 1991). During the 1980s it became clear that, because the majority of lone mothers were in receipt of means-tested benefits, they had little incentive to seek increased child maintenance, while piecemeal reform of the mechanisms for recovering maintenance from separated fathers was unlikely to make those mechanisms significantly more efficient (Maclean and Eekelaar 1993).

Policy context

A duty to provide child maintenance had therefore existed long before the CSA, but the precise extent of that duty and its enforcement lay ultimately within the discretion of the courts. In 1990 the government issued a White Paper with the uncontroversial title *Children Come First* (DSS 1990), in which the provisions of the CSA were outlined. The White Paper complained that the present system of child maintenance was 'unnecessarily fragmented, uncertain in its results, slow and ineffective'; and 'only 30 per cent of lone mothers and 3 per cent of lone fathers receive regular maintenance for their children', while 'more than 750,000 lone parents depend on income support [the main British social assistance benefit]'. The objectives of the CSA were to ensure that:

> parents honour their responsibilities to their children whenever they can afford to do so; a fair and reasonable balance is struck between the liable parent's responsibilities for all the children he or she is liable to maintain; the system produces fair and consistent results; maintenance payments are reviewed regularly to reflect changes in circumstances; parents' incentives to work are maintained; the public receive an efficient service; dependence on income support is reduced (*ibid*: Vol.1, p.i).

These objectives need to be set in the context of first, social and demographic changes and second, the Conservative government's general approach to social security policy.

Within the course of a generation family and household structures had undergone a radical transformation. Between the 1970s and the 1990s the number of lone parent families in Britain more than doubled and, as a proportion of all families with children, lone parent families had increased from 8 per cent in 1971 to 19 per cent in 1991. In the late 1980s, 90 per cent of those lone parents were women, of whom the majority (55 per cent) were divorced or separated, and 29 per cent were single (never married) (Burghes 1993). The proportion of single mothers appears to have been increasing, but research conducted in 1989 indicated that around 18 per cent of single lone parents had cohabited prior to becoming lone parents and probably had more in common with divorced/separated lone parents than with that minority of lone parents who had never cohabited (Bradshaw and Millar 1991). Increasing numbers of men and women cohabit without getting married and an increasing number of children are born to such couples. More marriages are ending in divorce, although many of those who divorce go on to live with a new partner or to marry. The point, therefore, is that lone parenthood is characteristically temporary, and the average 'episode' lasts around 3 to 5 years (Burghes 1993). None the less, only about a half of all British children can expect to spend the whole of their childhood in a 'conventional' family with a biological mother and father who are married to each other (Clarke 1989).

The impact on social security spending was considerable. Around seven out of ten lone parents at any one time were claiming income support, while the proportion of parents on income support who were receiving maintenance had fallen from 50 per cent in 1979 to 23 per cent in 1989 (DSS 1990: para.1.5, vol.1). The level of regular maintenance payments was low: the modal (i.e. most frequent) payment was just £10 per week per child. The then Chief Executive of the Child Support Agency made clear that 'the highest priority for the Agency is to change that culture ...... we are at the forefront here of a major social change' (SSC 1993: 8, 20). The very intensity of opposition to the CSA has been attributed by the government to 'the magnitude of the changes in attitude and practice needed if parents are to recognise that the primary responsibility for supporting their children rests with them rather than the state' (DSS 1995: 11).

The other context in which the CSA must be set is that of the Conservatives' long-term approach to social security provision. Since 1979 a distinctive feature of government policy has been, not merely to try and contain the growth of social security expenditure, but where possible to 'privatise' benefit provision (O'Higgins 1984; Papadakis and Taylor-Gooby 1987: ch.4; Dean 1993). 'Privatisation' has taken various forms. The introduction of statutory sick pay and statutory maternity pay 'privatised' the administration (and in due course the costs) of short-term sickness and maternity benefits by transferring responsibility from the national insurance scheme to employers. In a less direct way the reduction in the scope of the state earnings related pension scheme and the promotion through subsidies of personal pension plans and new occupational pension schemes effected a partial 'privatisation' of pensions by provoking a shift from state pensions to private pensions. In this context, the introduction of the child support scheme may be understood as another form of 'privatisation', on a par for example with the withdrawal of automatic entitlement to social assistance benefits from 16 and 17 years olds which forced many young people into private dependency upon their families. The CSA sought, not only to reduce benefit spending (by a target of £530 million in its first year of operation rising eventually to £900 million each year), but to pass the cost of sustaining lone parent and other low income families from the state to 'absent' parents as private individuals.

Outline of the scheme

Before addressing the issues which the CSA has raised it is necessary to have a rudimentary grasp of the workings of the child support scheme. An accurate and comprehensive explanation is provided, for example, by Garnham and Knights (1994a), but here a highly simplified outline is provided.

At the heart of the scheme lies the formula, a five stage calculation of the liability of the 'absent parent' (normally the father). The **first** stage involves the calculation of the *maintenance requirement* of the 'qualifying child(ren)' whom the absent parent is liable to maintain. The requirement is based on the currently prevailing income support allowances for each such child, but also includes an allowance for the 'parent with care' (normally the mother). This 'parent as carer' element has been portrayed by the government, not as a form of spousal maintenance, but as a part of the necessary care costs of children (DSS 1990). The **second** stage relates to *exempt income*, the minimum day-to-day living expenses which the absent parent must meet before being required to pay child maintenance. Once again, the calculation is based on current income support allowances, including provision for any of the absent parent's own children who may be living with him (but not for a new partner or any step-children with whom he may be living) and for personal housing costs (but not for the costs arising from any other liability or debt). The **third** stage relates to *assessable income*, the amount of the absent parent's income which remains after exempt income is taken into account. Absent parents with no assessable income may still be required to make a minimum payment, though some absent parents who are themselves on social security benefits or on very low incomes are exempt (if, for example, they themselves have the care of dependent children, or they are sick or disabled). The **fourth** stage produces the *proposed maintenance* which the absent parent is expected to pay. An absent parent pays 50 per cent of his assessable income towards the satisfaction of the maintenance requirement. If the requirement is satisfied before he has paid 50 per cent, then he is required to pay additional maintenance, based on a calculation which takes account of the assessable income of the parent with care and is also subject to an upper limit. The **fifth** and final stage relates to *protected income* and can reduce the absent parent's maintenance bill so as to ensure that his income and that of his 'second family' (if any) does not fall beneath a level set slightly above that of income support. Only at this stage will the requirements (and the income) of any new partner or step-children be taken into account. Changes to the scheme made in April 1995 additionally ensure that no absent parent will be assessed to pay more that 30 per cent of his normal net income in child support (DSS 1995).

The application of this formula rests upon another set of rules governing the machinery of the Child Support Agency and, for parents in receipt of benefits, the Social Security Benefits Agency. The Child Support Agency is responsible for conducting assessments of liability, the processing of applications, the pursuit of enquiries and the exercise of powers of collection and enforcement. Any parent with care of a qualifying child who is (or is a member of a household that is) in receipt of income support, family credit or disability working allowance is required to make an application for maintenance via the Child Support Agency, although the administrative 'take on' of some such cases has at the time of writing been temporarily deferred. Parents with care who fail to co-operate, by refusing to apply or by withholding information concerning absent parents, are subject to a 'benefit penalty' (a reduction of benefit lasting 18 months) unless they can show 'good cause' upon the grounds that the pursuit of the absent parent would risk harm or undue distress to her or the child(ren) concerned. These provisions attracted considerable criticism prior to the scheme's implementation. Parents not in receipt of benefits are not compelled to avail themselves of the 'services' of the Child Support Agency. However, once a parent applies for an assessment to be carried out the powers of the Agency to require information and to demand and recover payment (for example, through the attachment of earnings or benefits, or applications for distraint or committal) are brought into play and the rulings of the Agency take precedence over any pre-existing order by the courts.

The scheme is to be phased in so as eventually to apply to all child maintenance arrangements (i.e. regardless of the current marital and benefit status of the parents involved). It is estimated that the scheme could regulate the lives of some 10 million people. The government has now moderated the speed at which the scheme is to be introduced and additionally proposes legislation by which to allow some limited flexibility. It is proposed that from 1997 it will be possible for discretionary departures to be made from the formula, but only exceptionally and in cases where hardship or unfairness arises (DSS 1995).

Ideological controversy

The child support scheme was therefore a practical response both to social change and to the Conservatives' privatisation agenda. In ideological terms, such reform was fraught with ambiguity. I have already begun in Chapter 1 to discuss how 'the family' as an ideological construct has a contradictory appeal, both to the right (see Mount 1982) and the left (see Lasch 1977) of the political spectrum, while feminists remain fundamentally divided over issues relating to family and parenthood (see Williams 1989: ch.3). This is a theme to which this book will return, but in this chapter we shall see how that ambiguity was reflected in controversy over the child support scheme.

The scheme was conceived during the premiership of Margaret Thatcher, a clear exponent 'neo-conservative pro-familism' (Roche 1992). Introducing the child support proposals she declared that 'parenthood is for life' (*Independent* 19.7.90), echoing one of the tenets of an agenda for the family and welfare once enshrined in the report of an influential working seminar of leading US neo-conservatives (Novak *et al* 1987). Their concern was with the duties rather than the rights of parents, especially the duties of males to support the children they father. This was seen, not merely as a personal responsibility, but as part of a wider network of social obligations; a view reflected in the British social security secretary's declaration that 'it is no more acceptable for a caring parent to choose not to seek maintenance that for an absent parent simply to choose not to pay it' (*Hansard* 29.10.90, col. 731). The blueprint for the British proposal was in part inspired by an American scheme designed under 1984 Congressional legislation for the state of Wisconsin (which also influenced Australia's rather less rigid child support scheme - see Millar 1994).

The intellectual tradition to which the legislation gave expression has complex resonances and was presented in the US as the basis for a 'new consensus'; a pro-family policy which gave primacy to the family, which encouraged the 'bourgeois' (two parent) family form, which valorised the role of women as carers and men as providers, and which - in certain spheres - empowered families and parents against professionals and the state (Roche 1992: 110-22). Murray, one of the American political theorists directly consulted by British ministers and a leading participant in the abovementioned working seminar on family policy, has linked ideological assumptions regarding the role of patriarchal providers to ideas about the maintenance of social order: 'Supporting a family is a central means for a man to prove to himself that he is a "*mensch*". Men who do not support families find other ways to prove that they are men, which tend to take various destructive forms' (1990: 22). Amongst the remedies which Murray would offer are the withdrawal of state support for lone mothers and increased penalties for violent crime.

The contradiction of this ideological stance is that ensuring the autonomy of families from the state may also require intervention by the state to define and enforce the obligations of family members to each other. One might have expected that the neo-liberal wing of the political Right would have resisted such interference into the private affairs of families, yet it appears they have been swayed by neo-conservative leanings in favour of the enforcement of parental responsibilities and the strengthening of the patriarchal family. Just as Gamble (1988) argues that the New Right agenda required a free market supported by a strong state, so it also required self-sufficient families supported by a regulatory state. As a result, Brown (1992: 172) suggests, far from generating a new consensus, the rough consensus in family policy which had existed in Britain in previous decades has been destroyed.

None the less, a curious alliance has been forged between the Right and so called 'ethical' socialists. The Institute of Economic Affairs has been the unlikely publisher of a paper with a foreword by A.H.Halsey which bemoans the decline of the 'traditional' family and, in particular, of the role of fatherhood. Advanced capitalism, it is argued, risks producing a new breed of young male who no longer 'feels the pressure his father and grandfather and previous generations of males felt to be a responsible adult in a functioning community' (Dennis and Erdos 1993: xiii). While the IEA's Director blames the behaviour of men who opt out of familial obligation upon the existence of the welfare state (Green 1991), Halsey blames the tendency towards economic rationality and egotistical individualism promoted by free-market policies. Neo-liberal free-market philosophy and neo-conservative pro-familism represent, not opposite sides of the same ideological coin, but mutually incompatible components of a self-destructive political project.

Upon what might be called the 'soft left', one might have thought there would be resistance to an attempt apparently to 'privatise' social security provision for lone-parents. In the event, that resistance appears to have been outweighed by the 'ethical' view of parental responsibility or by a sense that the child support proposals were consistent with social justice. Labour MPs supported the child support scheme through its legislative stages. The proposals were critically scrutinised but ultimately welcomed by the Social Security Committee, chaired by Labour's veteran anti-poverty campaigner, Frank Field (SSC 1991a and 1991b).

It is not necessary to subscribe to an ideology of the family to be concerned about men 'opting out' of parental responsibilities. As Joshi puts it:

> The price a man pays for parenthood is generally being expected to support his children and their mother. The price a woman pays is that of continuing economic handicap and an increased risk of poverty. One of the many

> advantages of being male is that it is easier to opt out of the obligation to care. (1992:124)

From this perspective, the issue has less to do with the supposed efficacy of a particular family form as with the injustice of women's disadvantage. In spite of this, feminist commentators have been divided over the merits of the CSA between those who believe it serves to empower women and punish men, and those who believe it serves to perpetuate patriarchal domination.

Polly Toynbee (1994) has castigated the feminist left for its confusion and claims the child support scheme casts the Conservative government in an unfamiliar role as champion of women's rights. The scheme she claims not only represents 'the only big idea the Government has in its moral locker', but signals 'the biggest redistribution of wealth in [women's] favour since the Married Women's Property Act of 1882 gave them power over their own money'. This view ignores the widely held conclusion that the redistribution which the scheme was calculated to achieve was to the Treasury rather than to women (see Garnham and Knights 1994b). However, Toynbee articulates an ideological stance which not only justifies a direct redistribution of wealth, but the deliberate punishment of men for irresponsible procreation.

From an alternative version of the feminist perspective it is owned that 'this focus on child support does nothing to compensate for the real inequalities that marriage and child-rearing brings': on the contrary, '... the financial dependency of individual women on individual men is maintained' (Millar 1992:159). The fundamental problem is not that of coercing men into stable relationships with women or even into the acceptance of financial responsibility for children. The issue is structural. Women's disadvantage stems from their systematic exclusion from full citizenship (Lister 1990) though this in turn reflects the sexual division of labour and the way in which women's identities are constructed through their obligation to care (Graham 1983). As Land and Rose put it, 'altruistic practices are structured into women's lives as they are structured out of men's' (1985: 93). Collective provision by the welfare state has served to effect a measure of redistribution from men to women (Pascall 1986), but the assumptions upon which much welfare policy is predicated and the failure to guarantee genuine equality of opportunity have in fact contributed to the 'moral hazard' which enables men to avoid care-work while obliging women to do it for them (Taylor-Gooby 1991: 204). From this perspective, the child support scheme may exacerbate rather than lessen 'moral hazard'. The scheme is a development of the 'liable relative' provisions of previous social security regimes which themselves reinforced a structural division between caring and paying for children. The scheme enforces arrangements in which only one parent (preponderantly the mother) has responsibility for the care of a child and must depend upon the other to pay for this.

The scheme in practice

This chapter is concerned, less with the legislative technicalities of child support than with its wider effects first, upon income redistribution; second, upon women's dependency; and third, upon the way people behave.

Redistribution

The essential nature of the scheme is that it is likely to impose maintenance bills which, as a proportion of income, are greater for absent parents with low incomes than for those who are better-off. While this is mitigated by the protected income provisions, the effect can be to impoverish any new or 'second' family in which the absent parent might be established. The first Chief Executive of the Child Support Agency recognised that, as between 'first' and 'second' families, 'there is a redistribution of income here which is implicit in the legislation' (SSC 1993: 12).

This raises two points. First, because lone parents on income support have child support deducted pound for pound from their benefit, the redistribution which occurs is not to the parent with care, it is merely from the absent parent. Second, any resulting hardship or difficult budgetary choices do not bear entirely upon the absent parent, but also upon his new partner and any children in their care. Women generally command less of the 'family' income than men (Glendinning and Millar 1992: 8) and this is as likely to apply in 'second' families as in 'original' or 'first' families. What is more, there is evidence to suggest that it is in lower income families that women exercise a greater degree of management (though not necessarily control) over money (Pahl 1989). Where sacrifices are made within households, the brunt is normally borne by women, who will generally put the welfare of children and even partners before their own (see also Bradshaw and Holmes 1989). The redistribution that is involved as a result of the CSA may punish women in 'second' families rather more than it does men and is likely to lead to more rather than fewer women and children in poverty.

Dependency

This leads directly to another consideration, that of the child support scheme's impact on women's dependency. There are three factors here: first, the scheme requires mothers in receipt of benefits to co-operate with applications against the fathers of their children; second, it has allowed, in appearance at least, an overlap between child maintenance and 'spousal' maintenance; and third, on balance, it does little to assist mothers to achieve effective independence.

Statistics for the Agency's first year of operation reveal it had considered 65,000 cases in relation to the 'requirement to co-operate' provision (almost 8 per cent of the cases in which applications had been received). Of the 46,900 cases it had resolved, in 32,000 the Agency had accepted that harm or undue distress might be caused; in 14,200 parents were persuaded to co-operate; and in 700 benefit penalties had been imposed (CSA 1994: 11). However, NACAB and CPAG suggest that such figures do not tell the full story. Parents with care often co-operate only with reluctance and some, not understanding the rules, have withdrawn their benefit claims altogether rather than pursue maintenance (NACAB 1994: 79; Garnham and Knights 1994b: 109-11).

So far as lone mothers are concerned, those in Bradshaw and Millar's study (1991) felt by and large that the best thing about being a lone parent was a sense of 'independence' (the worst thing was 'loneliness'). Being compelled to (re-)establish financial dependency upon an ex-partner is clearly calculated to erode such independence at a subjective level, if not indeed more tangibly. Pahl's (1989) investigation of financial arrangements between men and women in marriage provides persuasive evidence of the extent to which female 'carers' (as spenders of household budgets) may bear the burden of managing, but male 'providers' (as earners of the household income) are likely to exercise ultimate control over spending. Once the tie between married or cohabiting partners has been severed the male provider's capacity for control is also broken, unless or until he is required to pay maintenance. Absent fathers interviewed in Bradshaw and Millar's study (*op. cit.*) all indicated that they did not regard the payment of maintenance as unconditional. Evidence from research conducted into lone-parents' initial attitudes to the CSA confirmed that the reluctance of some mothers to pursue maintenance is related to a fear that, with the payment of maintenance, comes a right of control over how such money is spent (Clarke *et al* 1993). Similarly, NACAB (1994) cites evidence to suggest that parents with care often fear that demands for maintenance (or for increased maintenance) from an ex-partner may result in unwanted intrusions to their lives and the lives of their children (or else that existing arrangements for contact and child access might be disrupted).

This is compounded by the inclusion in the first stage of the child support formula of the 'parent as carer' element, reflecting indirectly the requirements of the parent with care, rather than the child or children themselves. The presence of this element in the maintenance requirement may fuel the reluctance of some separated fathers to pay. It is also likely to fuel a woman's sense that she is personally dependent on an individual man; that she is bound by a form of private dependency (Garnham and Knights 1994b: 93).

Against this possibility must be weighed the idea that a state mediated maintenance settlement, or 'portable income', will provide women with a degree of security and independence and make it easier for them to break free of benefit dependency and/or to break into employment. This represented one of the government's main justifications for the scheme. The CSA included provision for various changes to the benefits system, namely the provision of a £15 per week child support disregard for lone parents on family credit (but not income support) and the reduction from 24 to 16 in the number of hours work per week which disqualifies a claimant from income support but entitles them to family credit. Coupled with this was provision in the November 1993 Budget for a £40 per week earnings disregard against child care costs for lone-parent family credit claimants. Additional changes now planned will permit parents with care receiving income support (or the related means-tested jobseeker's allowance) to have a deferred £5 per week disregard or credit against their child support which may accumulate but will only become payable as a lump sum if and when they subsequently take employment of more than 16 hours per week. The clear intention is to wean as many lone-parents as possible off reliance on social assistance (income support) and into low paid employment subvented by a means-tested in-work benefit (family credit). Such a strategy, however, does not lift lone-parents out of poverty, it is unlikely to give them much week-to-week financial security, and it takes no account of the shortage of adequate and affordable child care (Millar 1992: 160). For lone-parents remaining on income support, the absence of any (or any immediate) child support disregard means they are in fact no better off as a result of the child support scheme and, in the case of those whose child support lifts their income marginally above the income support entitlement level, they may be worse off as a consequence of losing entitlement to incidental benefits, such as free school meals. The only significant gainers from the scheme will be those lone parents who were financially better off to start with (Morris and Wasoff 1994).

Changing behaviour

The child support scheme is potentially damaging to women's independence, both symbolically and materially. It would also seem to stand little chance of changing the behaviour of men; or at least, the resistance strategies which are likely to emerge in response to the scheme are unlikely to benefit women or children.

A belated concession by the government provides for an allowance at the second stage of the child support formula for the notional value of 'clean break' property transfers made before 1993 by absent parents to parents with care. However, the effect of the formula is otherwise to exclude consideration of such settlements between ex-partners, and to demote the responsibilities which an absent parent may have assumed in relation to a 'new' or 'second' family. To this extent, the government has responded to recent changes in social life and family patterns by attempting as Millar puts it '.... to freeze the changes - to hold things still or even, if it could be achieved, to turn the clock back' (1993: x).

In the 1980s the allowance by the courts of 'clean break' divorce settlements gave legal expression to social changes favouring greater flexibility in the formation, dissolution and reformation of families and relationships. The principle involved was that, upon divorce, one partner (in practice invariably the husband) would make over to the other a capital sum or his share of the equity in the matrimonial home, in return for which he would thereafter pay no (or substantially reduced) spousal maintenance (though maintenance for children was in principle excluded from the provisions governing 'clean breaks'). The advantage claimed was that this provided a secure and permanent home for the woman and the children of the marriage; it left the man less encumbered by a continuing maintenance liability; and it allowed either for a more complete severance of the relationship, or else for continued contact between the parties and access to children without the acrimony often associated with subsequent reviews of property and maintenance arrangements. The legislation which opened the door to clean break settlements, the 1984 Matrimonial and Family Proceedings Act, had originally been promoted as a way to ensure that spousal maintenance should not become a woman's 'meal ticket' for life. The CSA has been seen as representing a step back from that principle but, in defence of this, the social security minister reaffirmed that '.... property transfers should not have been used as a way to avoid maintenance payments for the child' (SSC 1993: 31). Although the CSA's power retrospectively to negate arrangements already sanctioned by the courts has been modified, the clear intention remains. Clean break settlements perhaps symbolised the way that people expected and wanted divorce to work, but the effect of the CSA will be to frustrate such popular aspirations.

Changing expectations of marriage and family relationships are also reflected in the way people feel about second (and subsequent) marriages and about reconstituted or step-families. The clear signal given by the workings of the child support formula is that responsibilities to second families and step-children are inferior and secondary to responsibilities to 'first' families and 'natural' children. This is not necessarily the way that people feel about family relationships. The CSA represents a quite explicit attempt at 'social engineering'; at changing what people think and do (Finch 1989a). History suggests, however, that whenever in the past government has attempted to impose particular patterns of family obligation these have been resisted if they did not accord with what people think reasonable.

Of working age social security claimants interviewed in research by this author soon after the social security reforms of 1988, two thirds disapproved of reforms which might incline people to turn more to their families in preference to the state, or else they felt there were limits to what was acceptable in this regard (Dean and Taylor-Gooby 1992). For the parents amongst these claimants, parental responsibilities were seen as relating to caring in a non-material sense while, in the last resort, it was the state which was thought to be responsible for guaranteeing the financial security of the nuclear family unit; for enabling parents to care. These claimants aspired to mainstream cultural values which prize 'the family' in its individual nuclear manifestation for its affective relationships and emotional rewards rather than as a source of economic support. The implication appeared to be that policies which seek to impose financial obligations upon or within families are running against the grain of popular expectations; they risk undermining or deflecting the very things which people value about contemporary family relationships. In seeking to influence socially constructed life-cycle patterns the child support scheme goes much further than the social security changes of the 1980s, not least because it will also directly affect the lives of people who are not dependent on social security.

The first in-depth research on the impact of the CSA (Clarke *et al* 1994) was unable to find that any benefits (financial or emotional) had accrued to the children in the families studied, and reported in some instances that children were suffering because of the damaging effects which the CSA was having on relationships between former partners. The research confirmed much which was widely known or suspected about the impact of the CSA, about the consequences of the inflexibility of the original child support formula, and about the administrative failings of the Child Support Agency. It also drew attention to the ways in which the CSA had made relationships between mothers, fathers and children more difficult. Children had often experienced a reduction in their quality of life. Sometimes this was because of the disruption caused to informal maintenance arrangements (whereby an 'absent' father might regularly provide clothes, treats or presents). Sometimes it was because of reduced contact or increased friction between 'first' and 'second' families. However, the clearest overall finding was that

> The diversity of family structures reflected in the lives of interviewees suggests that distinctions between 'first' and 'second' families and between birth and step-parent relationships may be much less clear and much more fluid than the simple categories assumed by the CSA. (ibid: 5)

If there is to be popular resistance against the CSA, what form might this take? The collaborative strategies used by families against the 1834 Poor Law or the household means-test of the 1930s (see Finch 1989b) would seem to offer no model. It is possible for the mothers of qualifying children to avoid disruption to the equilibrium of their lives by accepting the 'benefit penalty' and this some women have already elected to do (NACAB 1994). It is however a strategy of submission rather than resistance. It was always more likely that it would be men who would seek ways to evade or minimise their liabilities under the Act, albeit in ways which will be of mutual benefit neither to their former partners and children, nor necessarily to their 'second' families.

One widely prophesied strategy is that men who cannot afford increased maintenance bills will simply give up work and become unemployed. Some men, in pique or desperation, may make dramatic gestures of this nature (even suicides have been blamed on the operation of the CSA). In the longer term, the effects on work incentives of expecting absent parents individually to pay higher levels of child support are likely to be more gradual and insidious. Ironically, Conservative governments have claimed that high marginal tax rates represent a disincentive to enterprise and so have sought to reduce income tax. The CSA entails the imposition of what is in effect an additional individual tax on absent parents so as to meet the costs of children fathered in previous relationships. It is structured like a tax (Chamberlain 1993 cited in Garnham and Knights 1994b) and indeed is proving an unpopular tax which, like the Poll Tax before it, some men may refuse to pay. Before the government's recent concessions, the Director of the National Council for One Parent Families claimed that fathers were 'on strike' and that the Child Support Agency was paralysed by the scale of their rebellion (BBC television interview, 17.5.94). More probably, however, men with high child support liabilities will have less incentive to work and, as 'traditional' male full-time employment contracts (Hewitt 1993), they may well just drop out of the labour market.

It is not inconceivable that the CSA could become just one more factor in what Therborn (1989) describes as a 'Brazilianisation scenario' whereby the UK economy is increasingly characterised by the casualisation of labour and extreme social polarisation. Potentially, there is another irony here. Moser has argued that 'women in the UK can learn much from their better organised sisters in the Third World, who long ago learnt the limitations of relying on the state to reduce their dependence on men' (1989: 184). If in the future neither the state nor men will provide support for children, then British women may be forced to increase their independence through self-help solutions; through reliance on low paid part-time work and collaborative community networks in which men play little or no part. Resistance to the CSA could contribute to the emergence of poverty stricken matrifocal communities in which women shoulder all responsibility and men are marginalised drones.

The alternative response to the incentives created by the CSA is precisely that desired by the government, namely that men may simply refuse to leave their partners' homes after the breakdown of a relationship, locking women and children into dependent and potentially damaging long-term relationships.

Conclusion

This chapter has only speculated about that which the child support scheme might portend. Time, experience and further research will no doubt provide clearer answers. Political developments are already altering the scope and nature of the scheme. Emerging from the analysis, however, are two key conclusions.

First, there are fundamental difficulties with a scheme which privileges biological parenthood over socially constructed parenthood. The idea that parents' moral duties to biological offspring are unconditional is an ideological contention which sits ill with the prevailing direction of social change and reproductive technology.

Western society increasingly recognises that the quality of parental care and familial relationships may be more important than the existence of a genetic relationship (for a helpful discussion of the significance of the 'blood tie' see Fox-Harding 1991). It is necessary to recognise the extent to which family responsibilities are socially negotiated (Finch and Mason 1992)

Secondly, any understanding of the implications arising from the scheme must take account of the gendered nature of parenthood. The CSA is constructed, without regard to gender, in the language of 'parents with care' and 'absent parents'. Debate both in and out of Parliament has tended by convention to assign the female pronoun to the former and the male to the latter, but it is explicit that this legislation should apply equally to parents of either sex. Most criticism of the Act never reaches the underlying principles which this conceals and leaves untouched the different consequences which the legislation has for women as a whole than for men. NACAB for example calls for '[a] fairer balance .... to be struck between the interests of parents with care, absent parents and other tax payers for the overall benefit of children' (1994: 107). For CPAG, Garnham and Knights more explicitly contend that the 'interests [of children] have been given lip-service in the current scheme while those of the tax-payer have been given prominence' (1994b: 143) and they argue persuasively that tackling the causes of child poverty requires a greater role for the state. I would not disagree, but would still contend that this is not so much a question of 'balance', as of the way in which relationships between men, women, children and the state are constructed; of the nature of the sexual division of labour and the potential of state intervention to either perpetuate or change it. It is about how the essential care-work which constitutes parenthood is defined, allocated and supported and about how social policy can influence that process.

I am grateful to David Berridge for helpful comments upon an earlier draft of this chapter.

3 Families in need: Crisis and responsibility

David Berridge

Family life today is closely scrutinised. Sociologists, depending on their predispositions, see the family as a key institution for the transmission of status, norms and values in society; a means for the socialisation of the young; and/or an agent of coercion and repression. Legislators and media commentators, especially on the political Right, frequently berate the social changes in family life. There is more divorce; partners choose to cohabit rather than marry; an increasing number of children are born outside marriage; there has been a rise in lone parenthood; more women also work outside of the home; and the arrival of children is often significantly postponed. A wide range of social ills is often, rather conveniently, attributed to these changes by the same commentators. These include the activities of children and young people and range from disrespect for authority, delinquency, and attendance and performance at school. It can also be felt to embrace neglect and abuse of the young.

This chapter continues to explore the central themes of this book by focusing on families at one extreme of experience. That is families, and specifically those with children[1], faced with extreme adversity. We refer to such families as 'families in need' and by this we mean those in which the health or development of children is seriously jeopardised ('children in need'). This language and conceptualisation is consistent with the Children Act 1989 (Department of Health 1989), which is discussed in detail later in the chapter. Families in need will also include those in which children

[1] The term 'children' is used in this chapter to include children and young people up to the age of 18 years, unless stated otherwise.

are suffering, or are likely to suffer, significant harm, including violence or exploitation.

Local authorities, fronted by social services departments, have a legal obligation to provide services and support for such families in crisis. Their exact circumstances will differ considerably but they will contain physically and emotionally deprived babies and the difficult adolescents many will eventually become. A large proportion of households will be headed by lone mothers trying to cope with extreme poverty and inadequate, often temporary, accommodation. Male violence, drugs and criminality may have been evident and, unsurprisingly, mental health problems are not uncommon. No doubt exacerbated by the context in which they were living, serious neglect as well as emotional and physical abuse of children are frequent. Sexual abuse is also increasingly being recognised. For some families, difficulties erupt during adolescence when sons or daughters are felt to be beyond control and getting into trouble.

Children in these circumstances will often remain living at home assisted, it is to be hoped, by social workers. However, where matters are particularly serious, children will be 'looked after' or 'accommodated' by the local authority. This can arise either with the agreement of parents or following a court order. The latest statistics reveal that, at any one time, there are over 50,000 children in England and Wales looked after, most of whom live with foster carers and some in residential homes (Department of Health and Welsh Office, 1994). As a proportion of the child population, this constitutes about one in every 200 but it reaches as many as one in 50 in inner London Boroughs (Department of Health 1993). There are also over 32,000 children listed on child abuse registers who have been, or are felt to be at risk of, abuse (Department of Health and Welsh Office 1994).

Such experiences form a very inauspicious start to life. The overwhelming majority of children and young people eventually return to birth parents (Bullock, Little and Millham 1993). Continuing, structured contact with absent parents is also mostly beneficial (Millham *et al*, 1985). However, those remaining in public care until late adolescence often leave without educational qualifications, have limited success in finding paid employment and too many have a series of unsatisfactory transitory experiences. Between one in seven and one in four female care leavers in two recent studies were already parents themselves (Garnett 1992; Biehal *et al* 1992). The 'cycle of disadvantage' theory, which was popular in the 1970s, was found to be too deterministic and disadvantaged social groups do not simply and automatically reproduce themselves over time (Rutter and Madge, 1976). Nevertheless, research has demonstrated that adults who were themselves brought up in public care often continued to have significant problems well into later life (Quinton and Rutter 1984).

In this chapter, therefore, we shall examine issues of parental obligations to children in the crisis circumstances outlined above, where family breakdown is threatened. We shall analyse how current social policy envisages parental duties in these circumstances. This clearly impinges on discussions about the boundaries between family and state, and whether welfare is perceived as benign intervention or a more coercive instrument (see Frost and Stein, 1989). In line with a central thesis of this book we shall also explore if, in relation to families and children in need, there has been a discouragement of centralised state provision and growing emphasis on family resources.

We shall see that the roots of policy in this area are complex and, unlike many areas, overt ideological influence is more difficult to discern. Indeed, the process and nature of recent reform is perhaps even unique for social policy in this country over the past 15 years. If so, it will be interesting to try to identify contributory factors. This evidence will also need somehow to be taken into account in developing general theory about the social policy process.

In order to understand the present context - including the situation, perception and responsibilities of birth parents in families in need - we can not totally ignore the historical origins of existing services. Current approaches and arrangements have long historical antecedents, which have exerted a significant influence. Few policy makers or professionals today would publicly espouse such harsh attitudes as existed in the past to the poorest in society and those felt to be negligent parents. However, more subtle influences can persist. There are several good historical accounts of child welfare services in England (see Frost and Stein *op cit*: ch. 3). Indeed, these also demonstrate how the notion of 'childhood' is far from fixed but is socially constructed.

Five main themes, relevant to the focus of this book, emerge from a review of the historical origins of child care services. First, it is apparent that concern with children's welfare is a recent phenomenon. The most significant developments date from only this century, for example the separation of child and adult offenders, and the removal of children from the workhouses. Secondly, it is evident that many of the responses to the problems posed by the poorest sections of society were extremely harsh and intended to provide a punitive deterrent to others not to transgress. Towards the end of the eighteenth century, it is reported that a majority of infants died in the workhouses. Hours of work were also excessive for pauper children. Stigma and discrimination were applied to unmarried women.

A third theme from reviewing the historical literature is that problems were attempted to be solved by separation of children from parents and their removal away from their place of origins. Child emigration was common to the outer reaches of the British Empire. Fourthly, families were seen as contaminating influences on children and any deficiencies were located within the parents rather than in their economic and social experience. Finally, and particularly relevant for the topic of this book, the attitudes and explanations of parents, and sense of their own responsibilities, were irrelevant considerations. Little account was taken of individual circumstances. The social problem to be dealt with was the threat to public order posed by members of the lowest social class; and the cure to this was seen as the redistribution of their children, both socially and geographically.

We shall see later in this chapter that these factors have continued to exert an influence more recently.

The remainder of this chapter is divided into three main parts. Initially, we examine different conceptual approaches to the situation of families and children in need. We then consider the major relevant legislation in England, the Children Act 1989 and its background. Finally, we end with some general conclusions.

Conceptual approaches to the problems of families and children in need

In such a complex and controversial area, it comes as no surprise to learn that contrasting perspectives have been developed to understand the situations, and possible responses to, families and children in need. These have been brought together by Fox Harding (1991), who developed a four-fold typology. Each of these has a specific approach to issues such as the nature of family problems, the responsibilities of the state, and the rights of adults and children. The four perspectives are described as: *laissez-faire and patriarchy*; *state paternalism and child protection*; *the modern defence of birth family and parents' rights*; and *children's rights and child liberation.* We shall briefly explore each of these in turn.

Laissez-faire and patriarchy

This first perspective is associated with a nineteenth century viewpoint but is also consistent with some recent observations. Broadly, it adopts a view that the state should play as minimal a role as possible in family life and the authority of parents should not be undermined. 'Patriarchy' refers to the sympathy with male supremacy over women and children in the family.

This perspective reflects a certain mistrust of the activities of the state and a tendency to suspect unwarranted intrusion. Family life is seen as overwhelmingly private and, apart from extreme cases, there is no general reason for the state apparatus to intervene. The family can also assume something of a romantic quality. Thus, there is a tendency to accept the status quo and power imbalances within families, notably the power of men and the subservient position of women and children.

One of the main groups of authors, according to Fox Harding, associated with the laissez-faire tradition are Goldstein, Freud and Solnit (1973; 1980). In their work, they argue that the child's needs must be paramount. Drawing on psychoanalytic theory, they emphasise the importance of continuity in relationships and the psychological needs of the child. These are best served, wherever possible, by professionals leaving families well alone. However, where family breakdown does occur, decisions should quickly be taken and this may entail children being removed to live permanently with alternative carers. This second family should then be accorded the same privacy and freedom from interference.

Others who have been linked with a laissez-faire perspective include those who have advocated more of a 'justice' approach, with an emphasis on civil liberties. This includes Morris *et al* (1980) and Taylor, Lacey and Bracken (1980).

It is tempting to associate the laissez-faire perspective with the political Right but this would not apply to all authors. Regarding the perception of birth parents, this approach would appear to assume a rather benign approach on the part of adults. It does not envisage a significant network of support services; and parents, it appears, should be allowed to act independently and are largely capable of doing so. Indeed, more of a problem is suggested as stemming from professional intervention rather than with the deficiencies in family life it is intended to address. Finally, by emphasising psychological rather than biological bonds with children, birth parents - paradoxically perhaps - ultimately do not have such strong rights regarding the care of their children as this perspective may initially appear to offer.

State paternalism and child protection

In contrast to the previous position, this perspective envisages a much more interventionist approach from the state towards children's welfare. It has a stronger belief that parenting is not always adequate and sets higher standards for family life than under *laissez-faire*. There is greater recognition of the position of children in society: they should be protected, and their welfare enhanced, wherever possible. However, although children's rights are emphasised from this point of view, they are seen essentially as dependent and in need of protection; this is in contrast to the greater right to self-determination that we shall see in the fourth model.

Therefore, this perspective places greater responsibility and confidence in the state and the abilities of professionals than *laissez-faire*. The state is not only obliged to intervene more readily but has the ability to act to enhance the welfare of the child. Courts and social workers are felt to be competent and their assessments insightful. Alternative family placements are highly valued, particularly adoption, and their problems understated. Similarly, the possible authoritarian and controlling acts of the state may not be acknowledged in the belief that welfare agencies act in the best interests of children and families. This may be problematic when, for example, there are gender or ethnic dimensions to decisions. Another way of approaching this perspective may be from a 'child rescue' viewpoint, which we saw earlier has been significant in the historical development of child welfare services in this country.

Fox Harding lists a number of authors who have written from a state paternalism/child protection perspective. Among them is Kellmer Pringle (1974), founder of the National Children's Bureau, who was critical of society's tendency to put parents before children and to consign too frequently the latter to unrewarding families. There should be a programme of parenting education to enhance children's life chances, and resources invested in preventive work to help struggling families. However, children are not the property of parents, she argued, and the tie should be cut if their development was unsatisfactory.

Other authors felt to approach child welfare from this perspective include Tizard (1977), who advocated the benefits of adoption. There is also Rowe and Lamberts' (1973) study, which highlighted large numbers of children languishing in public (mostly residential) care without clear future plans being made for them. It was argued that either greater efforts should have been made to return them to their original families, or alternative homes found. These ideas were influential on child care policy and legislation in the 1970s, including the 1975 Children Act and the development of 'permanency planning' approaches.

In contrast to *laissez-faire*, therefore, parental rights under state paternalism/child protection are much less significant and the welfare needs of the child justify more frequent state intervention. Parents have a clear duty to care for children but this is conditional on their acting in children's interests. Society's main responsibility is to children rather than adults. It is not easy to label politically this approach. At one extreme, high levels of policing of families would require major resources and numerous welfare bureaucrats. Alternatively, if separation were to occur, substitute family placements can be cheaper than many other options, especially adoption. It can also bring about a redistribution of children from the poor to the rich.

Defence of birth family and parents' rights

This third perspective we shall consider to the problems of families and children in need is more sympathetic to birth families. It emphasises that the relationship between children and birth families is very important and should be maintained wherever possible. The blood tie is important and appropriate services, therefore, should be delivered. Even where separation has to occur, it is felt usually to be in children's interests to maintain contact. It is often structural problems that are felt to lie behind the major difficulties of families in need, including poverty, unemployment and unsatisfactory accommodation. The impact of class and disadvantages experienced by minority ethnic groups are also significant. Thus, adequate support services should be provided and it is a contravention of civil liberties for children to be removed from poor families where the major factor determining the quality of care offered is a lack of resources.

In contrast to other perspectives this approach, therefore, emphasises the significance of both psychological *and* biological bonds between children and birth parents. It also demonstrates the acute sense of loss and injustice experienced by involuntarily separated parents. There is some scepticism about the adequacy and impartiality of courts' and social workers' actions. Insufficient resources are invested to help prevent family breakdown from occurring.

Authors identified from within this tradition include Holman (1976), who has argued cogently about the link between poor quality parenting and deprivation, rather than more individualised explanations. There is felt to be an imbalance between resource directed at providing for children once separation has occurred, rather than aiming to thwart the family crisis in the first place. Moreover, once children enter the public care system, contacts with parents may be discouraged and the two parties become estranged. Frost and Stein (*op cit*), referred to earlier, also elaborate some of these structural and political factors relevant to child welfare.

It is evident, then, that this third approach is more favourable than others to the situation of birth parents. It highlights their *rights* as well as responsibilities and the extent to which these are frequently disregarded. Greater material and other support is required for families in need. However, some would argue there is a danger in the rights of parents overriding those of children - an issue with which the fourth and final perspective is very concerned.

Children's rights and child liberation

This approach emphasises the importance of children's own viewpoints and wishes. The child is an individual with his or her own rights, just the same as adults. Children should be able to express their own concerns and wishes, and not merely depend upon adults articulating these for them. Adherents to this perspective point out, as we stated earlier, that childhood is a socially constructed concept, not something that is biologically determined, and age-related restrictions are arbitrary. Indeed, confusing messages - not least for children and young people themselves - are conveyed by the different ages at which the young are felt to reach adult status: matters such as voting, marrying, driving a car and so on.

This perspective is seldom reflected in law and policy, although it is now acknowledged as we shall see later. Clearly it has far reaching implications, advocating a much greater degree of self-determination. This represents a very different conception of childhood, in which the young are seen as more competent than with the other three perspectives and not so very different from adults. Under this, the protective role of the State would be substantially reduced or even withdrawn. It would not intervene in the lives of citizens purely on the basis of age. Parenthood, according to this view, is reduced to a very subordinate role. Its main task is to assist children in achieving their wishes and goals.

A number of problems can be envisaged which would stem from the application of this philosophical viewpoint. To be fair, we should distinguish among writers in this tradition, between those who take ideas to their complete logical conclusion and others who argue for greater acknowledgement of children's feelings, wishes and involvement. But at face value, a full implementation of a children's rights and child liberation approach would not, presumably, differentiate between juvenile and adult offenders. It could also have implications for child protection.

Holt (1975) is an example of one of the more extreme advocates of the *children's rights and child liberation* tradition. Challenging contributions on children's rights issues have also been provided by Franklin (1986) and Freeman (1983c).

Implications of alternative perspectives for parental obligations

Having outlined Fox Harding's typology, let us now bring out the implications of each for the situation and responsibilities of parents. We saw that the first three perspectives acknowledge the need for support for parents, though this would be very limited under *laissez-faire*. These three would also prefer nuclear families to other arrangements; a *children's rights* approach, in contrast, sees the disadvantages of intimate family life and stresses the potential contribution of wider kinship and community groups. The *laissez-faire* and *state paternalism* schools emphasise psychological rather than biological parenting. *State paternalism* and *defence of birth family* positions are more optimistic about what state services can and should provide. The latter is obviously most pro-birth parent. It can be seen that the four perspectives represented in the literature provide very different interpretations of the rights of parents and children and the role of the state. With the possible exception of the third approach, they are primarily child-centred. None of the perspectives, reassuringly, gives adults unmitigated rights over children. Moreover, the obligations of parents are often implicit rather than explicit. Authors seem to have concentrated more on children's needs than parents' responsibilities: the latter has received only limited attention.

This may reflect the historical legacy of child welfare services, outlined earlier, in which there was often a focus on child *rescue* and *separation.* It may also be related to the fact that child care policies in this country are frequent but *family* policy is much less evident. Similarly, this may stem from society's ambivalence towards the problems of the poor. To speculate further, and very important for the focus of this book, it may also reflect a political and wider consensus that children's welfare - indeed survival - is unlikely to be enhanced if undue responsibility and burden is placed on parents. This may account for some of the unique elements of policy and law in this area, as we shall now see.

Recent law and policy for families and children in need - the Children Act 1989

In order to examine present attitudes towards parental responsibility in families in need, we shall now discuss the main current legislation in this area - the Children Act 1989. This was implemented in October 1991 together with nine associated comprehensive volumes of guidance. It aimed to provide a more coherent body of public and private law, as well as to address criticisms from the House of Commons Social Services Committee (1984), the Review of Child Care Law (DHSS 1985a) and political and public concern arising from the conduct of certain child abuse investigations, especially in Cleveland (1988: see below).

The main purpose of the Children Act was described as promoting and safeguarding the welfare of children (Department of Health 1989). In this it set out '...to protect children both from the harm which can arise from failures or abuse within the family and from the harm which can be caused by unwarranted intervention in their family life' (*ibid*: 5). Relevant to the themes of this book, it was recognised that children are best generally looked after within their families. The legislation contained a variety of important new measures. For example, the Act uses the term 'parental responsibility' rather than parental rights. This refers to the '...collection of duties, rights and authority which a parent has in respect of his *(sic)* child' (*ibid*: 1). Parental responsibility is retained when family breakdown occurs and parents should continue to play a full part in a child's upbringing.

Where the health or development of children is significantly impaired ('children in need'), local authorities have a duty to provide services to assist their welfare. This includes day care, family centres and services for families with children with disabilities to try to enable them to lead as normal lives as possible. The duty to assist includes other agencies, such as education, health and housing, and not just social services. Steps also must be taken to prevent children suffering neglect or ill-treatment. Where children need to be 'looked after' away from home, local authorities must provide appropriate accommodation, such as foster or residential care. Even where court orders exist, the local authority and parents both possess 'parental responsibility'. In cases of voluntary arrangements, 'partnership' between social services and parents is encouraged.

The Act prohibits a court from making an order unless it is satisfied that this will enhance the child's welfare: a curious insertion some might feel but understandable given the research evidence we shall present later. Administrative measures to restrict parents' access to children or powers of recovery were abolished. Instead, all cases go to court. Children themselves must be consulted over matters affecting them. Children will have their own legal representation at all local authority proceedings and courts will also generally appoint *guardians ad litem* to promote their interests. In addition, the law allows for children to bring certain legal actions themselves. In decisions affecting them, local authorities must also take into account children's religious persuasion, racial origin, cultural and linguistic background. Complaints procedures have to be developed by local authorities and publicised to parents, children and other service users.

The Children Act introduced the fresh notion of *likely* significant harm as grounds also for legal intervention. However, emergency powers to remove children from home were reduced: in duration, emergency protection orders will last for eight days rather than the previous 28 (courts can grant an extension), and they are also subject to legal challenge from parents or children. Local authorities have a duty to advise and a power to assist young people up to the age of 21 who were looked after by them. In addition, responsibility was clarified for the welfare of children living away from home in a range of other settings, such as nursing homes and boarding schools. Significantly, the Act also introduced regular inspections of independent mainstream boarding schools.

There are many other important measures in the Children Act 1989 and its associated guidance. How are we to interpret these steps? What implications does it have for the responsibilities of parents and the role of the state? How does it fit into the conceptual framework outlined earlier? How does this legislation resemble other social policy legislation over the past 15 years?

The reforms and their ideological underpinning have been interpreted differently. Some observers might interpret certain measures as consistent with other recent Conservative legislation, discussed in this book, to place greater responsibilities on families and reduce or 'target' welfare services. For example, there is much emphasis on the new concept of parental *responsibility*, which makes it clear who is ultimately accountable and reinforces the fact that parents should not and cannot withdraw from the care of the young. Indeed, *responsibility* is highlighted rather than *rights*, and this is likely to have been politically attractive. The notion of 'partnership' with parents, in principle, might also be perceived as allowing for the diminution of state involvement in crisis circumstances and greater responsibility being forced onto families.

The same might be alleged for the reduced emergency powers, which could leave families to cope alone when in crisis. There is frequent mention of the need to avoid unwarranted intrusion in families, a theme also stressed in the revised version of *Working Together* (Home Office and others 1991), which provides guidance on procedures for the protection of children. Indeed, this is the first point that is emphasised in the opening paragraph of the report.

On financial grounds, the Act states that local authorities may charge for certain services; this does not apply to individuals receiving income support or family credit. Some have also claimed that many of the enabling measures are actually meaningless, as the government did not face up to the full financial consequences of the legislation and local authorities, therefore, were in no position effectively to implement it. Finally, critics of the Children Act have argued that a number of the measures did not go far enough: it often grants *powers* rather than obligations, and requires authorities to *assist* and *advise* rather than provide tangible services or financial help. There was unsuccessful lobbying on issues such as day care and aftercare, for example, which tried to get the government to commit itself further than it was prepared.

Parton (1991) has provided a stimulating contribution to the analysis of child care and child protection policy and practice in the 1980s, including a detailed chronology of developments leading up to the Children Act and its passage through Parliament. His theoretical approach is based on Foucault, considering disciplinary mechanisms in society and the changing nature of social regulation, particularly affecting family life. He also argues that social work itself was refashioned, as greater elements of legalism were introduced. His overall assessment of the Children Act 1989 appears ambivalent. While identifying distinctive qualities, he seems to believe nonetheless that there are many consistencies with wider social policy and other contemporary political initiatives. For example, he concluded:

> However it is important not to exaggerate either the significance or potential of these social democratic elements because, as we have seen, in other respects, particularly the emphasis on legalism and dangerousness, the changes are quite consistent with recent policy. (Parton 1991: 209)

In contrast, a more optimistic evaluation of the Act will be proposed here. It is suggested that the legislation, given the prevailing political context, was very forward thinking in much of its content and was even probably unique in social policy reforms over the past 15 years. In retrospect, the Children Act was a very skilful and subtle piece of legislation with apparently something in it for everyone. It did not herald a major transfer of responsibilities to parents, nor a diminution in the role of the state; if anything, potentially, the opposite. Its essential components were formulated more from within professional child care thinking than Right wing think tanks or the Treasury. This interpretation is more comparable to that developed by Packman and Jordan (1991).

Elements of the Act, mentioned earlier, would clearly appeal to and appease certain ideologues. However, the bulk of its measures seem to be intended more to support families and strengthen the rights of parents and children. Indeed, Fox Harding (*op cit*), though the legislation was in its infancy at the time, locates it essentially within her *defence of birth families and parents' rights* perspective. For example, the Children Act extends preventive powers; stipulates responsibilities towards a wider group of 'children in need'; makes it a legal obligation for different agencies to collaborate with social services; strengthens the legal rights of parents in conflict with social services; rationalises the court structure and tries to reduce delay; and enforces complaints procedures within local authorities.

In addition, the Act is very child-centred in its orientation and contains some radical measures. Children's views are to be taken into account; the importance of ethnicity and culture are explicitly recognised; children themselves are to be separately represented in court and can bring certain actions; services for children with disabilities are brought into the mainstream; and independent schools are to be regularly inspected by social services - a remarkable encroachment into the lives of the middle- and upper classes (but not for long, see below!). There are also important elements, therefore, sympathetic to a *children's rights* perspective.

Perhaps even more importantly than its actual content, the Children Act is notable for what it does *not* contain. It was introduced by a government during a period in which business principles and market forces were being applied to many areas of social policy, including the community care reforms which were proceeding simultaneously through Parliament (NHS and Community Care Act 1990). Yet the Act displays virtually none of these exhortations. There are no explicit references to privatisation. There is also no mention of the 'purchaser-provider' split so cherished elsewhere. The rhetoric of consumer 'choice' is also absent. As with the somewhat ironic feature of the community care reforms, local authorities remain the central agency. A key role for professionals is also preserved: indeed even *social workers*, apparently not one of the government's most valued groups or strongest supporters. It is also striking that children themselves are at centre stage of the legislation; and though one might after all expect this from a *Children* Act, the same could be said about recent education reforms, which are more geared to parents' concerns rather than pupils (for example the Education (Reform) Act 1988). Parents, rather than children, are now consumers of education.

In all, then, it is felt that the Children Act 1989 was unlike any other major social policy legislation of the 1980s. Its contents are virtually unique in recent history, both for what it does, but also what it does *not*, contain. It has little resemblance to other developments in education, health, housing or penal policy. In particular, it does not signify a major increase in family obligations and a diminution in the role of the state.

The Act was also unique in that its key messages were based on, and consistent with, a solid body of child care research: unlike probably reforms in any of the other areas of social policy mentioned above Therefore, some of the measures that might be interpreted as shifting responsibility to parents (and were probably astutely presented in this light), in fact are more likely to be responses to criticisms highlighted by researchers about the imbalance of power between agencies and parents, and the insensitivity and ineffectiveness of some social work activity.

An influential summary of nine major child care research studies (Department of Health and Social Security 1985b) made for disquieting reading and clearly required urgent remedies. This was one important strand leading up to the need for, and shape of, new legislation. It revealed that too many social work decisions with families and children in need were unplanned and made in crisis. Compulsory powers tended to be used routinely and inappropriately and were often counter-productive. Parents' perspectives were unrecognised and they felt neglected. Social workers did not always recognise or acknowledge the stresses parents had undergone. They were often relieved when children entered public care but social workers frequently misinterpreted this as *rejection* (Fisher *et al* 1986). For those children separated from their parents, maintaining contact could be problematic and was often not encouraged (Millham *et al*, 1985). Therefore, very relevant for the themes of this book, parents often wanted to exercise more responsibility but were prevented from doing so by professionals - the opposite of what one would find in other areas of policy. Moreover, foster and residential placements were too often unstable, which could compound original problems. It can be seen that a number of the legal reforms outlined earlier are seeking to address some of these deficiencies.

Several of these concerns were relevant to events occurring in Cleveland in 1987 where, over a six-month period, some 125 children were diagnosed as having been sexually abused by their parents, most children being removed from their homes. In contrast with some other child abuse crises, here it was paediatricians who came in for most criticism, their diagnoses perceived to have led to the children being prematurely and insensitively removed. These events, which received widespread public attention and condemnation, had a significant influence on the context leading up to the Children Act. They also helped shape attitudes to the balance of power between professionals and parents, and the respective rights of children and adults (see Parton *op cit* : ch. 4).

A pertinent question, which is difficult to answer, is why were the reforms regarding families in need so different from other areas of social policy? Why was there not the significant shift of responsibility to the family and away from the State, consistent with other political initiatives? How is it that notions of 'partnership', considerations of ethnicity, consultation with children, and letting loose social workers in prestigious boarding schools could be approved by this government? It has been proposed that the government's interests were predominantly elsewhere. This is a possibility although it seems unlikely given that delegation does not seem to have been one of the former Prime Minister's strongest points.

A number of ideas can be tentatively proposed. First, it has been suggested that 'children' is, or are, less of a political issue than most others. It is conceivable that discussions of child neglect and abuse, or death, tend to attract universal condemnation, which is likely to promote consensus. Party political debates on such issues could appear unedifying. Yet discussions of poverty and child benefit, which of course impinge very much on families in need, are highly political events. So, as will be seen in Chapter 4, is juvenile crime.

A second suggestion is the influence that *child abuse* considerations specifically had on the debates, especially events in Cleveland. Many politicians were preoccupied with this and were probably unaware of some of the wider issues. So long as these matters specifically were addressed, other more radical measures could be introduced. Indeed, some of the high profile responses, such as encouraging parental *responsibility* and deterring unwarranted intrusion in families, were politically attractive concepts.

Thirdly, and a more unusual element in social policy formulation, is that certain key individuals were highly influential to the process. This applies particularly to certain senior civil servants. These were well-informed, took an interest in research and communicated well with, and were respected by, professional groups. Consequently, when the Children Act went forward it did so with widespread endorsement: once again, something that is very unusual for recent social policy legislation.

Conclusion

Having covered some wide-ranging territory, let us now begin to draw this discussion to a close. First, we shall reiterate some of the main points already raised.

Our task has been to consider attitudes towards parental obligations regarding families and children in need and the related role of the state. We argued that a historical dimension could not be overlooked. We also outlined the conceptual framework developed by Fox Harding (*op cit*). This helped provide a theoretical understanding of child care problems. In a political context in which emphasis has frequently been towards a more minimal state, we saw that recent child care policy in fact has been in the direction of greater family support, as well as more adequate recognition of parents' and children's rights.

It was argued that the Children Act 1989, in many respects, is virtually unique in social policy over the past 15 years. It contains a number of measures that would appeal to the Right. However, essentially, it is a family- and child-centred piece of legislation which, in itself, does not signify a major shift in responsibilities to parents and away from the state; again, if anything, the reverse. Its measures were underpinned by a body of child care research. These studies demonstrated frequently that parents *wanted* to exercise greater responsibility but were *prevented* from doing so by the services that were provided: a different perspective from what one often finds.

Some analysts may be perplexed or even irritated by this overall argument, in which recent government social policy has been positively endorsed. It may partly stem from an intellectual approach which has sought to derive explanations and theory from the social world, rather than impose a cherished framework from the outset which will then determine the sorts of answers one gets. (It was Glaser and Strauss (1967) who described this cogently, if unkindly, as theorising from the data rather than the armchair.) But if it were to be thought that we are being complacent, we need finally to turn to the implementation of the Children Act and its reception. Here we shall see that matters are more problematic. The Act is still in its early days but this should, nevertheless, be sufficient to deduce some early lessons.

For the Children Act measures to have any success, we must obviously take into account the context in which it is introduced. An important area is the contentious one of resources. Governments and local authorities often disagree publicly about the adequacy, and even scale, of social services budgets. The former in recent years have been elected following proposals to restrain public expenditure; yet in politically sensitive areas such as health, education and social services, they have been reluctant to claim credit where this has been achieved. Given such controversy, it may be legitimate to turn to an independent and outside view. The US visitor Schorr (1992) has published his impressions of the current personal social services scene. His comments do not make encouraging reading. He concludes that for the past 15 years the personal social services have been severely underfunded. He also states that, in the financial year the Children Act 1989 was introduced (1991-2), a quarter of local authorities were budgeted to spend no more in real terms than the previous year despite its inception. The main conclusion is that 'Too much has been laid on an already overburdened service' (*ibid*: 3).

Another important part of the context into which the Children Act has been introduced is to consider what has happened to families economically, and incomes in particular. The main factor uniting families of children in need, who come to the attention of social services departments, is that they are usually desperately poor (Bebbington and Miles 1989). This has been consistent historically, as we saw. The middle classes, in contrast, choose to purchase alternative services and boarding schools are sometimes used when problems are acute (Anderson and Morgan,1987). Making a link with poverty is not to excuse the behaviour of adults who neglect or injure children. But it would seem obvious that depriving families of adequate financial resources is likely to exacerbate tensions and stress.

Here again the evidence is not favourable. Kumar (1993) has provided a major review of the literature concerning the effects of poverty and inequality on children in the UK. He demonstrates that child poverty has increased dramatically since 1979: the number of children affected has increased threefold from 10 per cent to over 30 per cent of the population. Another 10 per cent live on the margins of poverty. Poverty disproportionately affects children from minority ethnic groups. It was shown to have adverse consequences for children's health and education. These findings were reinforced by an authoritative report from the Joseph Rowntree Foundation (see Barclay 1995 and Hills 1995), which highlighted the growing inequality in Britain and its negative effects. It also argued that, between 1979-92, the poorest 20-30 per cent had failed to benefit from economic growth, in contrast to the rest of the post-war period.

This increase in poverty would be expected to add to the numbers and problems of children in need. It will be recalled that one of the innovative parts of the Children Act was to strengthen local authorities' responsibilities to provide services for this group. Has this emerged in practice? An early review of the implementation of the sections concerning support for children in need found a varied picture (Aldgate, Tunstill and McBeath 1993). Greater collaboration between agencies had occurred, as the legislation had intended, about setting policy and delivering services. However, the survey also discovered that authorities were concentrating mostly on children felt to be at risk of significant harm and frequently were overlooking the wider group of children in need. Consequently, there was insufficient preventive work undertaken to confront problems at an early stage. Agencies responded that they would have preferred to have offered this service but that resource constraints prevented it.

Since the implementation of the Act, certain of its measures have also come under pressure. Some early adjustments had already been made to staffing ratios in day care settings. Registration criteria are being revised to enable childminders to smack children where parents permit it, which is seen to be at odds with the general Children Act philosophy. There has also been a fascinating instance of class interests reasserting themselves and social services' powers of inspection over boarding schools are being significantly diminished. This is despite early evidence that most schools found the experience beneficial and child protection concerns were not uncommon. At least the situation affecting *special* boarding schools for pupils with statements of special educational need will remain unaltered.

Although these are the problem areas, we should not overlook the positive achievements. Early impressions are that the Act mostly is being implemented and practitioners find it a better structure than before. Fewer children are being looked after by local authorities and it may be that working in partnership with families is managing to circumvent the need for separation (Department of Health and Welsh Office, 1994). There was also initial evidence of a drop in numbers on Child Protection Registers, although it remains to be seen how future trends develop. Less use is being made of emergency powers without, it appears, adverse consequences. In addition, despite the fact that practice could improve significantly, many areas have made progress in involving more effectively young people themselves in plans and decisions.

So we end this chapter on a mixed note. The Children Act 1989 was unparalleled among recent social policy legislation. It was child- and family-centred and did not seek to transfer significant responsibility to parents away from the state. It also sought to remedy some of the power imbalances that have been present in services over a long period. Some critics may feel it was over-optimistic and unrealistic, given that it is being implemented in the financial and political context we have described above. Despite this it was a laudable achievement in an otherwise hostile period and an important symbolic statement about the experiences of families and children in need.

The author is grateful for comments on an earlier draft of this chapter from Leoarna Allen, Isabelle Brodie, Hartley Dean, Rupert Hughes, John Paley and Mike Stein.

4 Troublesome children: Failure and moral liability

Brynna Kroll and David Barrett

Your children are not your children,
They come through you but not from you,
And though they are with you yet they belong not to you,
You may give them your love but not your thoughts,
For they have their own thoughts,
You may strive to be like them but seek not to make them like you....
You are the bows from which your children as living arrows are sent forth.

Kahlil Gibran (1923) *The Prophet*

As these lines indicate, the relationship between children and parents is very complicated in terms of 'ownership' and the ways in which similarities and differences are managed. Who owns children? Are they objects or subjects of concern - possessions or individuals in their own right? What does 'controlling' children mean and whose responsibility is it? What part do parents and state play and what is the potential for working together; for the kind of 'partnership' that, within the context of the 1989 Children Act (already discussed in Chapter 3), has become the key word in relationships between children, parents and state agencies? Who regulates the degree to which parents actually do control their children? Can this be done by the internal regulatory systems provided by families themselves, or must external powers be brought into play in the form of welfare services, or control via the education system or the community at large?

When it comes to dealing with young people who are troublesome, recent debates have focused on the need to 'listen less and punish more'. This suggests that listening actually used to form part of the process which took place between young people and those adults (whoever they were) whose responsibility it was to care for them. Such catch phrases, however, do little to take the debate further forward. It is these very issues of control, responsibility, dependence and independence, as they are played out in the justice system, that will form the substance of this discussion. We shall examine many of the conflicts, contradictions and tensions that are associated with controlling children within such a system. The justice system has provided and continues to provide a focus for many of these debates about who is responsible for young offenders. Here we use the justice system as a point from which to chart where the pendulum of responsibility swings.

In this chapter we shall first examine the concept of parenthood and the moral problem of troublesome youth. These issues will be illustrated in relation to a prominent case with which the justice system has recently dealt and which encapsulates several aspects of current controversy. We shall then explore the balance and debates between the 'just deserts' and the 'welfare' approaches within the youth justice system (Rutter and Giller 1983; Parker *et al* 1989), including some very recent changes in legislation, before returning to the issue of responsibility. We conclude with some analysis of the balance between duties, responsibilities and rights. Within this approach the following associated areas will also be considered: the rhetoric associated with justice debates; tensions within the justice system; and the uncertainty about who is in the dock in the youth court, the parent or child?

It was a wise judge who once observed about children in the justice system that they are especially vulnerable because they do not have the developed defences that adults have and therefore need special attention (Levy 1994). When our criminal justice system is observed it appears that this reasonable premise is too frequently ignored.

Concepts of parenthood

In considering these issues, inevitable questions arise about the nature of parenthood and the art - for this indeed is what it is - of parenting itself. Children are produced for all kinds of complicated reasons. As a society, we rarely obtain any important item of worth without reading the operating manual before hand; children are the exception to this rule. It is only when they arrive that we wonder how they work and what to do with them (Pugh and De'Ath 1989). We need to fashion them in a certain way because they are part of us and we therefore make a whole range of assumptions about what and, more importantly, who they are like. Children who go 'bad' or 'wrong' confront parents with something very profound within themselves with which they must tangle. Children who express violent, passionate, destructive feelings and who do violent and destructive things - or even simply naughty things - can cause despair, frustration and murderous rage in even the most liberal and enlightened breast. When we yell at our children, we are actually projecting onto them our own feelings of guilt for getting it wrong. This is the proof of our shortcomings as adults. One hour in a busy park or supermarket will demonstrate that children's capacity to threaten the mortality of others - 'I'll kill you if you don't shut up!' - is learnt at a parent's knee. Perhaps, as Miller (1987) argues, we simply get the children we deserve.

When things go wrong, then, in terms of children coming before the courts, it is the parents who need to be both understood and listened to, as well as their offspring. In this context the courts can be seen as some kind of legal guardian to a 'good enough parent', to use Winnicott's immortal phrase (Winnicott 1965; Adcock and White 1985). From the central perspective that the welfare of the child is paramount, the court will dispense a just penalty, support and maintain the parent's authority, and balance the arguments from all sides. What actually happens, however, may be very different and it is some of these tensions and the complex dynamics which accompany them that we want to consider.

In practice, the often contradictory roles expected of the court merely reflect contradictory conceptions of parenthood. As a society we are never quite sure whether troublesome children are to be dealt with as the villainous offspring of culpable parents or as the hapless victims of inadequate parents.

The moral problem of troublesome youth

We shall argue that, just because the law says that parents should be 'responsible', it does not mean that people understand what this means or are able to put it into practice. Parents are consistently told to take control of their children but many parents feel blamed and feel failures. Simply telling them is not sufficient to enable anything to change without an understanding of the complexity of people's lives and their experiences, both as children themselves, and as adults. The dialogue between the court, the parent and the young person is fraught with potential misunderstanding. Exchanges between magistrates and parents may evoke the long silenced voices of authority figures from the past, some of which may have been less helpful than others. Telling parents off, threatening them with fines or imprisonment, rather than entering into an exploration of the underlying issues does not encourage debate. Moral outrage as an end product is not constructive in itself (Stevenson 1993).

Indeed, debate could be positively dangerous. What it might reveal may not in fact be anything to do with personal pathology and wilfully wrong choices, which represent the cornerstones of the deterministic approach to wrong doing and of the 'just deserts' model at the heart of the Criminal Justice Acts of 1991 and 1993. It may instead consistently underline the role that structural inequality, racial discrimination, class oppression, poverty and disadvantage play in the lives of most of the young people who come before the courts, and in the lives of those who care for them (Pitts 1986 and 1988).

The 'prison works' argument reiterated most recently by the Home Secretary at the Conservative Party conference in September 1994 is a tidy way of dealing with the mess and muddles of peoples lives. This 'tough on crime' approach is symbolised by the imminent creation of secure training centres, despite the fact that the precursors of this innovation - the approved school, the community school with education, the detention centre, and the borstal - were all ultimately seen as failures.

Just about everyone has a view and opinion about young people and crime and whose fault it all is (West 1982). There was a time when young people were seen to 'grow out of crime' (Rutherford, 1986). Implicit in this argument was a belief that there was something else to grow into; a new stage of development marked by the establishment of stable relationships with partners, employment, parental responsibilities of their own, and so on. Recent arguments suggest, however, that due to economic changes, there is in fact nowhere to grow into, particularly for young men, who have lost a role and status that was thought to be due to them (Pitts 1990; Barclay 1995). Thus young men often find themselves still attached to the delinquent gangs that provided their *raison-d'être* as adolescents. The degree to which parental control can affect this state of affairs is hard to fathom (Freeman 1983a and 1983b). More recently the blame over who should instil discipline has been aimed at schools, social workers, parents, 'video nasties', the community - even the church has had its turn.

Prominent cases and issues

The tragic death in 1993 of four year old toddler, Jamie Bulger, caused by two ten year olds, Thompson and Venables, in Bootle on Merseyside, epitomises some of the issues and brings many of these debates to a head, despite the fact that not only was it unusual, but as some argue, also irrelevant to the debate (Cavadino 1994). The baying crowds outside the courts where the accused were tried simply replicated the murderous intent that they were condemning. As a society we were forced, if we could bear it, to look at the violent, primitive, destructive side of human nature that we would prefer to forget. Like others before them, these child killers were seen as 'bad seeds' rather than products of their environment. Their parents were judged, castigated and effectively hounded out of the community. The Norwegian town of Trondheim suffered a similar tragedy to that of James Bulger in October 1994; a five year old was beaten to death by three five and six year old boys. The community's reaction, however, was very different - ' the overriding reaction is one of forgiveness and people talk of the importance of bringing the boys into the community not victimising them' (*Observer* 23.10.94). This tells us something important about our society's need to project all its badness outwards rather than to own it and grapple with it.

The Bulger case brought home some harsh realisations. Some people do not look out for one another as families in the accepted way. Some people stand back, if you intervene you are damned, if you do not - the same. Be responsible only for number one! These issues have an impact on whether parents feel supported and therefore feel able to care for and sustain their children, and for children to develop a sense of responsibility. Do children look out for one another too? Parents need help with learning about control, and children need to have this modelled for them.

Much media and political attention has also been focused on young people involved in stealing cars and careering around housing estates at the expense of other law abiding citizens. The punishment versus treatment debate has been almost completely submerged by the ascendancy of a populist 'lock 'em up and throw away the key' philosophy. This is in spite of evidence that custodial sentences have been associated with reconviction rates of up to 80 per cent (Hagell and Newburn 1994). More recently the 'hooligans on holiday' scandal emerged: local authority social services departments were castigated by press and politicians for taking young offenders on adventure trips as part of their rehabilitative regimes. The furore arose despite the fact that only a tiny fraction of young offenders under supervision -

0.0004% - receive such treatment (*Guardian* 23.9.94). The new national standards for 'The Supervision of Offenders in the Community' (published in March 1995) reflect a curious obsession with anyone going anywhere, let alone on holiday, whilst under surveillance, lest it should appear that these young people are being rewarded for wrongdoing, although the emphasis on physical activity is seen as important.

A new language is evolving that includes such terms as 'ramraiders' and 'joyriding'. This is not unlike similar changes in language in the late 1970's, which saw the birth of the term 'muggers', for example (Hall *et al* 1978). Panic speak has now been extended to embrace the female of the species, so much on the periphery hitherto. Sexual equality, 1990s style, is reflected in the latest 'moral panic' - the upsurge of 'rude girl', juvenile female gangs on the rampage (*The Times* 25.11.94).

The effects of some of these newly defined phenomena have been profound. But what of establishing an informed view and opinion? There have been many changes in the way young offenders have been dealt with - some contradictory. Managing the changes brought on by growing up has never been easy as Shakespeare's shepherd observes:

> I would there were no age between ten and three and twenty,
> or that youth would sleep out the rest; for there is nothing in
> between but getting wenches with child, wronging the ancientry,
> stealing, fighting.
>
> *The Winter's Tale* (Act III, Scene III)

These clearly are sentiments with which Michael Howard, the current Home Secretary, and a host of parents, teachers and social workers would concur. The shepherd too has experienced the single parent moral panic, assaults on elderly people, and the more commonplace theft and violence. In short, youth has always been a problem; the solutions however must be grounded in the realities of the present day rather than based on illusions about the past.

Establishing an informed view and opinion is therefore complex. But we must continue to ask questions about the way we manage and treat young people. How do we treat young offenders? What should the response be to crime? Recently, tough measures have been demanded to stem what people see as the rising tide of crime but let us not forget about the spirit of the 1989 Children Act, although not aimed primarily at young offenders, it offers the 'child first' principle. This Act is also at an early stage in its life (Aldgate *et al*, 1994). Currently the pendulum is swinging towards punishment which is taking increasing precedence over welfare (Crisp 1994).

But what is the current position within the arena of youth justice? Two significant pieces of legislation have been passed in the 1990s, the Children Act 1989 and the Criminal Justice Act 1991 (subsequently amended by the 1993 Act). In order to understand the legal framework within which youth justice is enacted we need to consider how these two bedfellows are getting on together.

The youth justice system: the balance between 'just deserts' and 'welfare'

Bad or sad? This question, with two very dramatic images at its centre, is in many ways at the heart of the youth justice debate. As Cavadino and Dignan observe:

> On the one hand the image of the young 'thug' is the perennial focus for fear, hatred and 'moral panics'... and this sometimes leads to particularly punitive measures... On the other hand our attitudes to children in trouble can also be infected with the sentimentality evoked by children generally in our culture which can lead to less punitive measures being countenanced for them (1992: 201; see also Parsloe 1976; Harris 1985).

It is perhaps because of these contradictory images that the treatment of young people in the justice system has appeared contradictory in its turn. The history of the justice system could broadly be characterised as a range of attempts to balance notions of welfare and justice; the juvenile justice system has been no exception. The welfare model of justice, which has been heavily positivist, was rooted in the belief that people who broke the law did so due to some underlying problem whose roots lay in their individual pathology and once this has been 'diagnosed' it could then be 'treated'. Help rather than punishment was the order of the day. One of the major consequences of this was that if you were identified as one of the 'deserving' you could be 'sentenced' to social work for an indefinite period and thus become what has been called a victim of welfarism.

The justice model, in contrast, rests on the premise that all people who offend are rational beings capable of making decisions about what they should or should not do; as a consequence when they break the law they should be punished and ideally 'the punishment should fit the crime'. Essentially this model seeks almost literally to put an adult head on young shoulders, treating adolescents as rational actors. Although capable of modification by the 'maturity test', which enables young people's level of development and capacity for rational thought to be assessed (although how this is done is not clear), it is apparent that an adult schema is at the core of the philosophy. But disadvantage is often ignored here. For example, the experience of poverty, which correlates closely with the incidence of crime, may need to be weighed in the balance as a contributory if not a mitigating factor (Hills 1995). On the positive side, however, the just deserts principal is aimed at achieving two important goals: that like cases are treated alike and that an offender is punished for what he or she has done in the present, not for everything else that has gone before. The latter egalitarian principle has been undermined to some degree by the 1993 Criminal Justice Act, which has repealed Section 29 of the 1991 Act, in which that principle had been enshrined. As a consequence, all previous convictions are now taken into consideration when sentence is passed, somewhat undermining the idea of the punishment fitting the particular crime.

Changing approaches to justice

The journey that led to the Criminal Justice Acts of the 1990's is useful to explore, albeit briefly. Intervention by the courts between parents and their children was first sanctioned by the ancient common law doctrine of *parens patriae*, though this was customarily invoked only in relation to property matters and for the offspring of the propertied classes. It was not until the nineteenth century that attention turned to the social problems occasioned, on the one hand, by the destitute offspring of the 'perishing' classes and, on the other, by the delinquent offspring of the 'dangerous' classes (Morris *et al* 1980). The creation in 1908 of the juvenile court encompassed both these concerns, combining criminal and welfare jurisdictions in a single forum. The juvenile court was kept separate from the ordinary courts, but it was only in the 1930s that it began to develop its specialised nature, with specially appointed justices and distinctive rules of procedure and disposal. Troublesome children had become a cause for a special kind of intervention. By the 1960s doubts were being expressed about the compatibility of the juvenile court's criminal and welfare jurisdictions (Ingleby Report 1960).

The 1960s can be seen as an enlightened period in which, in stark contrast to the 1980s and the 1990s, thoughtful and progressive attempts were made to transform the juvenile justice system. Pitts sums it up this way:

> ...the reformers attempted ....to raise the age of criminal responsibility to 17, to transfer the control of juvenile justice from central to local government, and

> to abolish the imprisonment of children and young people... The reforms of the 1960's aimed to recast the image of the young offender as a victim of social deprivation and the psychological problems which such deprivation engendered. As such the young offender needed the scientifically informed interventions of 'trained experts' rather than punishment (1992: 172-3).

Underpinning this thinking were some important strands. First, there was an acknowledgement that deprivation and disadvantage actually existed and played a part in delinquent behaviour; the child was in fact a product of the environment and the state had a role to play in examining both the causes and consequences of social inequality. Secondly, it was recognised that the criminological concepts of labelling, stigma and deviancy amplification had a part to play. A court appearance was much more likely to confirm a young person in a deviant identity. The idea of help of a skilled nature rather than punishment, with its implications for decriminalisation, was pretty revolutionary. Unfortunately, revolution was not what Edward Heath's Conservative administration had in mind.

The problem with the tenets of what was to become the 1969 Children and Young Persons Act (albeit in a somewhat mutilated form) was that - rather like the 1991 Act - it threatened the power and autonomy of the sentencers. As a consequence, the more radical proposals were not implemented. The elements of a new system which had survived were simply bolted onto the old system - a piecemeal approach which left big loopholes. The age of criminal responsibility remained at 10 thus 'ensuring that the supply of delinquents was not diminished' (Pitts *op. cit.*).

The battle then between welfare and justice continued to rage. Ironically a piece of legislation which had hoped to divert young people from custody resulted in an increase in the use of imprisonment for juvenile offenders. In the years that followed, various initiatives were tried in an attempt to obtain valid alternatives which would provide surveillance as well as gainful activity in the community. Sentencers needed to be convinced that there was something out there which was tough enough to look like punishment and that worked. Intermediate Treatment therefore had to start to look like an alternative to custody. However, the roots of the problem - social disadvantage, inequality, poor support for struggling families - continued to stay where one might expect them; underground (Utting 1995).

We move now to the late 1970s and '80s. Sentencing policy under the first Thatcher administration did not lock up thousands of extra people, but the second administration let the prison population grow by one-sixth to a peak of nearly 50,000 in 1988. There followed a dramatic change of view: prison it seemed 'made bad people worse'.

This went to the centre of policy making so the prison population dropped to 42,000 in January 1993. Interestingly, as the public were fed with media stories of the younger generation being out of control the population of young offenders in custody actually dropped from 10,000 in 1981 to nearer 5,000 now, although those held for over six months has increased. However, influenced perhaps by political rhetoric, the current Home Secretary was busy overturning what could be described as a 'liberal' success in sentencing.

The economics of keeping people in custody was also revealed to be suspect with the whole expense of non-custodial sentences equalling the same as two weeks in custody, currently costing approximately £1,000 per week. The original 'do-gooders' had been liberal Victorians who were successful in their own way: at least they understood that there were other factors associated with crime like levels of poverty, employment prospects and the importance of positive welfare policies.

If the Tories' anti-crime policies are scrutinised more closely it is possible to identify a consistent approach to juvenile offending which developed both locally and nationally between 1982 and 1991. The nation's youth was not out of control and existing responses were not weak or inadequate. As Crisp comments (1984) 'the government's figures show its "developmental" approach of the 1980s evidenced through a series of Acts, circulars and initiatives between 1982 and 1991, was successful'. It appears the government was not prepared politically to take the credit for this major social policy achievement.

The seeds of a particular kind of thinking had in fact already been sown early in the 1980s. A 1980 White Paper asserted 'it is important that the courts should .... be able more effectively to bring home to parents their responsibilities in relation to children who offend' (Home Office 1980: para. 53). Accordingly, provisions were incorporated in the 1982 Criminal Justice Act by which to make parents accountable for their children's actions. Though provision already existed by which parents could be fined or ordered to pay compensation for offences committed by their children, the courts were placed under a stricter duty to consider their powers in this respect.

Meanwhile there was impetus for new legislation. This was in part motivated by the realisation that crime cost the country considerable sums of money and that locking people up was expensive, particularly when most of them did not actually pose a threat to the public. There was an awareness that sentencing practices were erratic and inconsistent and that there was not a sufficient distinction made between offences against the person and offences against property.

This provided the backdrop against which a new criminal justice emerged, based once again on just deserts.

By this stage another piece of innovative legislation had come into force, the 1989 Children Act. Born out of pressures on social work tasks of various kinds, its aim was to shift the balance of power from what were seen as extreme actions by social workers operating behind closed doors and making hasty and ill informed decisions concerning parents and their children, to a partnership between parents and social workers (DHSS 1985b). It made social workers more accountable for their decisions and introduced a range of new orders to protect children and ensure that appropriate steps were taken with the minimum of delay (Freeman 1992). In the context of this discussion the key elements of this Act which relate to the criminal legislation are the emphasis on the welfare of the child as being the paramount consideration, and the concept of parental responsibility. As Freeman points out,

> The shift from parental rights and duties to parental responsibility contains three messages. First that responsibility is more important than rights... Secondly it is parents and not children who are the decision makers ...Thirdly the emphasis on parental responsibility contains that all important message that it is parents and not the state that have responsibility for children (1992: 19).

The message to parents is clear. To borrow a slogan, 'children are for life and not just for Christmas'; you cannot wash your hands of them even if you want to and, when the going gets tough, you are on your own unless something really dreadful happens. We have only to consider the wider lives of Thompson and Venables to realise the true horror of this situation. Thompson and Venables were not educationally stimulated, secure, happy children with stress free lives. They were children living on the edges of society whose parents had experienced stress and difficulty in varying degrees.

It is alongside this that we come to consider the criminal legislation. The 1991 and 1993 Criminal Justice Acts have at their core this central idea of just deserts and proportionality. The 1991 Act in fact represented this idea in what could be termed its most pure form in that it enabled people to be sentenced only for the current offence without taking any previous convictions into account. However, the Act was rapidly judged to be a 'criminals charter' for this very reason. This provision, embodied in Section 29, was repealed by the 1993 Act. So much for just deserts! (Ames 1991). In the youth court, however, an element of the welfare model was retained. This means that some balance has to be achieved between the 'just deserts' principle, the welfare of the young person and their stage of development. In addition the note of parental responsibility embodied in the Children Act also comes into play in the legislation in as much as parents, guardians, or a local authority acting *in loco parentis* must attend if the young person is under 16 and can be bound over to ensure their offspring stops offending. Here we see a significant shift towards bringing parents centre stage (one that is increasing with recent suggestions that parents can be fined up to £1,000 if their children do not comply with orders made). In the days of the 1969 Act parents were frequently present in court to show their concern or to present a good front; they tended to be viewed sympathetically by sentencers although a degree of censure was often apparent (*ibid*: 10). The message of the 1990s however seems to be different. Parents seem almost to be in the dock alongside their children; parenting is on trial and if you are found guilty of failing to do your job, to control your child, you will pay the price.

There is another criticism of the legislation. It is often perceived that families had much easier access to help than they do now. Under both criminal and child legislation, preventative initiatives were seen as acceptable, and anti-social or delinquent behaviour seen as a cry for help. A supervision order could be made sooner rather than later for relatively minor misdemeanours if it was apparent that there were significant welfare issues which could be addressed. Of course there are dangers here. As we said before the perils of being 'sentenced to social work' for years on end were very real; on the plus side, though, some useful diversionary work could be accomplished such as that of Intermediate Treatment schemes.

With the advent of the 1991 Act, however, supervision became reserved for offences which were 'serious enough' to justify a community penalty rather than made on the grounds of welfare needs alone. Thus by the time this point is reached there is a danger that behaviour and problems have become so entrenched that intervention may be less effective. To simplify, one could say that to have a social worker or a probation officer assigned to a case these days the position needs to be serious. Just as in child care, where the parents who can see disaster looming are turned away with a request to return when it actually happens, parents whose children embark on a criminal career in a minor way are left to their own devices, aided and abetted by the occasional caution, until a serious offence is committed. How helpful is this?

Matters are of course further complicated by the 1994 Criminal Justice and Public Order Act. The Home Secretary now appears to be back-tracking from alternatives to sending young people into custody.

Indeed, his 'prison works' philosophy will be responsible for the creation of more secure accommodation aimed at 12-14 year olds. More young offenders are finding their way inappropriately into children's homes too (Berridge, 1994). These practices and plans have received criticism from the United Nations in January 1995, following the first international audit of children's rights in Britain (Travis 1995). The UN accuses our ministers of repeatedly violating the UN Convention on the Rights of the Child, which the government signed up to four years ago. It also included other criticisms such as high levels of child poverty and teenage pregnancies.

The 1994 Criminal Justice and Public Order Act introduces a new sentencing measure, the secure training order, to deal with persistent young offenders. The order allows courts to consign offenders (guilty of three or more offences) to a secure training centre for a maximum of two years, half in detention and half under supervision. There will be 200 places offered by five privately run centres at a cost of between £2,000 and £3,000 per week per child. However, according to Home Office research there is no need for new secure training centres because the numbers of persistent young offenders do not warrant it. A survey of 33 police forces during a three month period in 1992 found only 106 cases of young people who had committed 10 or more offences (Adler 1994). Are they persistent enough? It has been alleged with some justification that the Criminal Justice and Public Order Act is a knee-jerk reaction to tabloid headlines heralding a crime wave of persistent young offenders. Is governmental control getting out of hand for reasons of political expediency?

Diversion from criminal activities has to be a part of alternatives to custody but proper systems for help and support are often lacking. A recent NACRO survey (1993) of social service departments found there was little in the way of support for children, or their parents, after a child had been cautioned for an offence. Similar gaps exist for young people on bail. Other commentators (Hagell and Newburn 1994) raise questions about whether most persistent offenders have to be locked up to protect the public, for their offences are rarely violent or sexual in nature.

Section 16 of the Criminal Justice and Public Order Act aims to increase the number of children receiving custodial sentences by including ten year olds in this category. This effective lowering of the age of criminal responsibility has not been debated thoroughly, as Frances Crook, the director of the Howard League, acknowledges (Crook 1994). This makes the age of criminal responsibility in England and Wales one of the lowest in Europe (Scotland 8, France 13, Germany, Italy and Austria 14). The age of criminal responsibility at common law was seven. In 1963 it was raised by statute to ten. In 1969 Parliament decided that generally, though not for homicide, it should be 14. Under the Criminal Justice Act of 1993 more custodial measures are available for younger children. For example, 'secure remands' will be available for children as young as 12. This is a harsher climate for young children (Crisp 1994).

Responsibility

It is sometimes difficult to establish exactly who the present Home Secretary is denouncing when he suggests that 'do-gooders' have 'too much influence over the criminal justice system' (Howard 1993). Currently, it seems, he can only mean the criminal justice system as represented by the judges, magistrates and civil servants who both know and run the system. Some of these conclude that although a rising crime rate is bad, a rising prison population is worse. All prison does, they would argue, is make offenders worse.

Politicians have responsibility too. The 'back to basics' theme discussed in Chapter 1 started a search for those to blame. This was directed primarily at parents but was particularly aimed at single mothers, non-maintenance paying fathers and, for example, the conduct of parents who allowed their children unrestricted access to adult videos. There was a great push to put responsibility back to parents. This was exemplified by the phenomenon of the 'home alone' syndrome'; a moral panic fuelled, especially at Christmas time, by the story line from a film on general release in 1993 and some well publicised instances of children being left by parents to fend at home for themselves. Moral outrage seemed to become an end in itself. Some of these initiatives back-fired. The Child Support Agency, for example, evoked such an adverse response from some sections of the public, that the Agency's Chief Executive, Ros Hepplewhite, resigned in early September 1994 (see Chapter 2 above). It might be argued that Hepplewhite became a scapegoat for a flawed piece of legislation.

Yet the lessons from previous positive policies are now being ignored. The Criminal Justice Act of 1991 has been seriously weakened by the amendments and, at the time of writing, the Criminal Justice and Public Order Act is about to reverse some of the earlier polices.

The present government appears to be on a self made justice roller coaster ride on which continual changes in direction are taking place. This is perhaps best demonstrated by the 1991 Act, which was changed almost as soon as it had become law. Lobbyists for the victims of crime were particularly skilled at putting pressure on the government. This was endorsed by reactive responses, not least political rhetoric for the purposes of gathering votes. For example, it was Michael Howard who recommended a minimum sentence of 15 years for the Bulger murderers (announced 22.7.94). Did he ignore or listen to the public mood? The Home Secretary received 21,281 coupons from readers of the *Sun* newspaper calling for a 'whole life tariff'. This recommendation has a 'Call of the Wild' mentality about it (Dyer and Bell 1994). Fifteen years is nearly double the eight years that the trial judge thought adequate and half as much again as the ten years the Lord Chief Justice thought right. Apart from the Irish Republic, Britain is the only country in the EU where a politician rather than a judge can pass sentence in such a case. It can also be argued that Britain is probably alone in being the only country where the term a prisoner serves can be partly determined by the readers of a tabloid newspaper.

The Home Secretary's involvement may evoke appeal procedures in this case because some legal opinion argues that public opinion is irrelevant. Under the terms of the European Convention on Human Rights, courts not politicians should determine sentences. There has in fact been a general decrease in the number of instances in which Home Secretaries have exceeded the tariff recommended by judges (from 57 in 1990 to 4 in 1994, Dyer and Bell 1994). This suggest that a very particular example was being made of the boys, Thompson and Venables. Generally, lighter sentences have been given to young people. The departure from the established norm in this case was perhaps an example of trying to make political mileage from a nightmare scenario.

Parents and children: duties, responsibilities and rights

The ability of parents to control their children is influenced by a number of factors. In order to have a sense of our duties, rights and responsibilities we need to have a useful model to follow, an understanding of the concepts, an ability to separate our needs from those of our children and a secure base from which to operate which gives us room to consider our children as separate but dependent individuals in their own right. There is, as we know, no such thing as a perfect parent but there is the idea of a 'good enough parent' and there is a sense that children have basic needs which must be met. The World Health Organisation checklist includes food, shelter, stimulation, affection. To this list we might add the provision of appropriate models for behavioural boundaries and of a sense of right, wrong and respect for others.

In order then to have a responsible child or young person we need a responsible adult. But how reasonable is it to expect responsibility in a child? Developmentally this is a task that takes many years to accomplish; it requires concentration and ability to focus. Whether this is something we can expect from a ten year old is debatable. Piaget (1932) originally contended that it was not until the age of eleven that children began to develop what he termed an 'autonomous morality'. Later theorists of child development paint a more complex picture. What we call 'maturity' in a democratic society involves a transition from mere obedience (obedience that is to the rules or constraints which are imposed by parental or other external authority) to responsibility based upon the acceptance of abstract principles. This transition takes time and we none of us achieve it in quite the same way.

What is more, the capacity for this kind of responsibility may be undermined by various external factors - poverty, misery, parental discord, bullying, lack of stimulation, unexplored intelligence. Such circumstances militate against parents giving children their full attention; keeping them in their mind; noticing when they are not 'okay'. On the one hand we know when a child is a child; on the other, when it comes to the commission of offences we expect an adult capacity, an old head on young shoulders. During the Venables/Thompson trial the media appeared shocked by the fact that each child lied to protect himself and shift the blame to the other. What eleven year old (they were eleven by the time the trial took place), would not do this faced with the enormity of the deed - indeed what eleven year old might not do this as a first resort faced with any minor accusation?

We need to accept that the state has a responsibility to support parents, educate young people to become parents and communicate the enormity of the task that lies ahead when you decide to produce another human being. This responsibility would then ideally be handed on from parent to child with each element of the system feeling supported by the other. We believe that when children do something terribly wrong as Thompson and Venables did it is because there is something terribly wrong somewhere in the system of which they are part and it is only by examining all parts of that system that we can understand and prevent it happening again. In Trondheim, Norway, as we have seen, they seem to have a more reasoned approach.

The background philosophy of a culture, the ideology underpinning social policy and the culture of the family are all linked together. In Britain 'the family' is a 'private' institution (Mills 1959). In France, for example, it is more open and 'public' (Cooper *et al* 1995). This means, as Cooper observes, that in the UK political responses to the family are characterised by a deep ambivalence because of the separateness of the state, the individual and families (*ibid*: 100). Therefore a tension exists and the possibility of real integrated responsibilities and partnerships are less likely.

The problem is for us all, but it is felt particularly by young people. As Crisp (1994) observes, concern has swung away from young people themselves towards the needs of those affected by their actions. John Major urged us to 'understand less, and condemn more'. We are not for a moment suggesting that victims of crime should not be accorded the same attention as perpetrators, but that consideration be given to the fact that children are often members of both camps. Those in positions of power do have responsibility to divert young people from delinquency and to keep people in their communities. This requires a government which gives priority to careers and jobs for young people; local authorities which value localised services; and people in localised neighbourhoods willing to support young people in their own community. All three have interdependent roles to play.

Children have rights too, as Wingham argues (1994), and have the right to be safe and understood. The 1989 Children Act reminded us all that the welfare of the child is paramount. We still do not seem to be any nearer to the notion that protecting children and guiding their growth, development and socialisation is the responsibility of everyone in the community.

Who is in control of children? The central state? Local authorities? Parents? Children themselves, or their advocates? The pendulum of responsibility will doubtless continue to swing until such time as the whole is understood rather than just the parts. Perhaps it is time to blame less and examine more.

5 Ethnicity, culture and parenthood: Policy dilemmas

Rah Fitches

> Not only is there a clash between some of our intuitions about fairness, but well meaning policies may well collide. (Modood 1994: 14)

This chapter raises questions first, to do with the extent to which policy intervention in relation to child rearing practices should be culturally sensitive, but second and more fundamentally, to do with the circumstances in which it is right that the state should intervene. Tariq Modood, in the statement quoted above, has opened an interesting debate which bears directly upon such issues. Modood argues that the 'vague multiculturalism' of prevailing policy ideology in Britain fails adequately to address the phenomenon he calls 'cultural racism', whose complex character 'cannot properly be defeated by the politics of religious harmony or by anti-colour-racism' (*ibid*: 7). For example, he draws particular attention to Muslims who, unlike Sikhs and Jews, have not been deemed to be an ethnic group and so are placed outside the terms of existing anti-discriminatory legislation. What is more, if ethnic norms, group solidarities and patterns of behaviour are to be endorsed in policy, it cannot be assumed that this will necessarily be consonant with a political culture of individual rights. Controversy about policies which allow Asian girls to be withdrawn from certain activities at school (such as sex education, sport, dance) is cited as an example.

As this chapter will make clear, social policy constructed within the paradigms of western European thinking may be seriously challenged by the child-rearing practices of other cultures. 'Progressive' social policy thinking, informed by insights both from feminism and anti-racism, may need to take stock when confronted, for example, by the highly gendered nature of child-rearing customs and practices in some ethnic communities. The chapter will briefly discuss general issues relating to the objectives of the recent Children Act before moving on to discuss first, the cultural specificity of family life and second, the provision of services for the children of ethnic communities. It will draw partly upon such literature as does exist, but mainly upon research carried out by the author with Bangladeshi families in Luton (see Fitches 1994).

By way of preliminary explanation, I should explain that that research was conducted on a modest scale and many of my findings should be regarded as speculative. The study was primarily concerned with the health beliefs of the Bangladeshi community, using the taxonomy constructed by Kleinman (1980). Kleinman distinguished between three categories of belief: folk beliefs, popular beliefs and professional beliefs. My study focused specifically upon a small sample of Bangladeshi families having children with learning difficulties. In the course of my investigation and the difficulties I encountered, a number of highly specific issues emerged. The Bangladeshis are a very traditional group, with a rich amalgam of cultural and religious influences (both Muslim and Hindu), and the potential for conflict between their beliefs and those of health care professionals was high. The needs and the existence of the Bangladeshi community was poorly recognised: their presence was not fully disclosed by census data, since many Bangladeshis had been inappropriately categorised in earlier censuses. Also, the Bangladeshis were comparatively recent immigrants and, in the locality I studied, it appeared they may have suffered particularly from isolation; from discrimination arising both from white racism and from the low esteem in which they seemed to be held by certain other more settled Asian groups; and from language barriers.

Child-rearing practices and the Children Act

Official guidance to the 1989 Children Act states:

> The needs of staff to work with families from the ethnic minority communities require particular attention. Cultural differences may present in different patterns of parenting and information about these must be made available to the staff concerned (DoH 1992: 9)

The 1989 Children Act, which was implemented in October 1991, was the latest in a succession of legislative provisions to be introduced within the last hundred years: the Prevention of Cruelty to Children Act of 1889; the Children Act of 1908; the Children and Young

Persons Act of 1933; the Children Act of 1948; the Children and Young Persons Act of 1963; the Children and Young Persons Act of 1968; the Children Act of 1975; the Childcare Act of 1980; and the Children and Young Persons (Amendment) Act of 1986. However, none of these Acts responded to the needs of the ethnic and immigrant groups that were settling in Britain. The issues of culture, religion and the other factors which influence how parents care for their children were never fully explored.

In spite of the good intentions expressed in the abovementioned policy guidance, discussion of legislative outcomes consistently fails to take on board the complexity of the issues. An independent working party established by the Department of Health in 1991 defines five different kinds of outcome to be anticipated from the implementation of the 1989 Children Act: public outcomes; service outcomes; professional outcomes; family outcomes; and child outcomes (G. Parker 1991: 20).

- At the level of *public outcomes*, legislation seeks to safeguard the health and safety of the nation's children, but also to safeguard family life from unwarranted interference by state agencies. There is unexplored scope for conflict here since, to use the example which has already been mentioned, the health of Asian girls might arguably be prejudiced if parental wishes regarding their exemption from physical exercise at school are respected.
- *Service outcomes* may have entirely different significance or meaning for different ethnic communities. In the Bengali language, for example, there are not even words to define physical 'disability', learning difficulties or 'mental handicap', phenomena whose existence is explained in ways which may defy 'scientific' western understanding. Services directed to alleviate the needs of disabled children or support children with difficulties may not be apprehended by Bengali parents as having any outcomes at all.
- At the level of *professional outcomes*, cultural differences in child-rearing practices can similarly give rise to conflict, when for example culturally specific ways of disciplining children may be interpreted by professional opinion as child abuse.
- For *family outcomes* to be measurable, it is necessary for families to have shared aspirations or common interests. Ethnic communities may resent services which impinge upon their family values and customs in which case outcomes may be unquantifiable or even negative.
- In terms of *child outcomes*, we have already seen in Chapter 3 that the Children Act makes the interest of the child paramount.

> Defining the interests of the child may, however, pose a dilemma in situations where child-rearing practices conform to the expectations of neither policy makers nor service providers.

Although Britain is now considered to be a multi-ethnic, multi-racial and multi-cultural society, there is still a long way to go to address all the issues raised by the presence of minority communities. The particular needs of such communities in relation to the care of children, and the restrictions imposed upon them are numerous, but there is very little literature in this area or evidence that there has been any attempt to understand differences in child-rearing practices. Concerns have been expressed by many of the agencies involved in child care, but concern alone is not evidence of awareness.

The cultural specificity of family life

Each society has a generational order in which adults (both men and women) have some kind of authority over children, though the nature of that order and the kind of authority that is exercised differs from one culture to another. This is hardly new. Kardiner, for example, states 'wherever we find .... organised collections of human beings, we find some habitual regularity and organisation of inter-relations among the various individuals. We find also organised ways of dealing with the outside world in order to derive from it satisfactions essential to life' (1989: 37). However, parenting also differs from culture to culture. Each culture has its own organised way of dealing with the processes of parenting and child care. Religion, values, customs and traditions all play a part. Where such patterns of organisation persist over time and are transmitted from generation to generation, we speak of a 'culture'. Such is the variation between cultures, however, that even the composition of basic 'cultural units' can differ: a cultural unit may include only immediate family members, or it may extend to include other relatives and kin, or even whole settlements or groups of people, such as applies in the case of the kibbutzim to be found in the state of Israel.

Burke and Dalrymple contend that 'parental responsibility does not mean that the child is property to be owned by any one person', rather they describe parental responsibility as 'all the rights, duties, powers, responsibilities and authority which by law a parent has in relation to the child and his [*sic*] property' (1991: 4). If parenting and parental responsibility are to be prescribed in this way, what consequences might this have for cultural minorities in Britain today? Very little attention has been paid to the parenting and childcare practices of ethnic communities, especially Asian communities. References are made in contrasting accounts by Sharma (1991) and Ahmed (1990) to caring and parenting issues amongst certain Asian communities, but much remains to be learned about the specific features of their respective cultures if the development of social policy is to be properly informed. Of particular interest to this author is the situation faced by recent immigrant groups, such as the Bangladeshis who only began to settle in Britain in significant numbers in the 1970s at the time of political upheavals in the South Asian sub-continent.

Gender and the 'political economy' of the household

Patriarchal authority and economic relations can be powerful influences upon the way children are cared for. This was very much so in the Bangladeshi families I studied, where an awareness of a gendered hierarchy, respect for elders and discipline was instilled in children from a very early age.

The majority of these children lived at home with parents and siblings. In almost all the cases the mothers were the principal carers. The only exception was a family in which primary responsibility for the care of a disabled child had fallen upon an older sister following the death of their mother. Day to day care was an almost exclusively female domain, and girls as young as seven would be expected to contribute to the upbringing and care of their siblings. The rearing of children was seen as a female role and, although the males within these families appeared generally loving and caring towards their children or siblings, they distanced themselves from the practicalities of care. Most members of these families contributed towards the upbringing of children, but there were clear and concise gender oriented rules on who did what. Mundane jobs were allocated to the females; matters of discipline and conformity to cultural tradition were instilled by the fathers or father figures, such as older brothers. This role would fall to the oldest male offspring (even if the oldest child in the family was female).

Girls were often kept at home to help with household chores and the care of younger siblings. This could have a disruptive effect on their schooling. Intervention by the local education authority could prove a source of conflict, since education for girls was not seen as a priority or necessity. Official pressure was sometimes circumvented by sending girls away for long periods to Pakistan or Bangladesh.

This was often explained by parents as a necessary measure for the girls to learn their own culture in preparation for marriage.

Female roles were enforced by male authority. Cooking, washing, ironing and caring for the family were seen as a routine for girls and refusal to contribute to these tasks would often lead to strict discipline by the fathers and older brothers. Many families believed that this is all a part of preparing girls for marriages which may take place when they are in their early teens. However, a failure to prepare girls for marriage is blamed on mothers.

Bangladeshis have traditionally had large families and hope to have more sons than daughters since this will secure the future of the family and ensures that parents will be cared for in later life. The tradition has been coupled with high infant mortality rates in Bangladesh, and with economic circumstances in which children are, because of their earning potential, an assurance to a better life. Contraceptive advice is often therefore ignored and represents a potential source of tension, being disapproved of by religious leaders and disparaged as an infringement of a husband's right to a larger family. The opinions of women are discounted.

Boys are considered as the jewels in the family crown. They are seen as providers for parents in their old age and an insurance policy for their futures. Girls, however, represent a future financial liability, since dowries (sometimes amounting to the equivalent of several years' earnings) are payable when they marry.

Delegation of parental responsibility

We have seen that, in the Luton Bangladeshi families I studied, girls but not boys were often obliged to participate in the provision of care for younger siblings. The extent to which such care was delegated was greater than that which applies in most western European households, but it did not signal any abrogation of responsibility on the part of mothers who were by and large totally dedicated to their role. Similarly, a father's responsibilities could be delegated to sons. In one family studied matters of discipline had been left with a sixteen year old son while his father was visiting relatives in Bangladesh. He could not cope with this role and often stayed away from home or pretended to be sick to avoid confrontations with his two older sisters.

Turning from Luton's Bangladeshi community in particular to Asian child care practices in general, it is worth saying something about another form of parental delegation that is instanced in informal types of fostering and adoption amongst groups from the South Asian subcontinent. Girls are more often the subject of these arrangements because they need to be provided with dowries when they marry. If there is more then one daughter in a family, this can represent a considerable liability. Adoptions whether informal or formal can therefore help the financial situation of a family and is often welcomed. Many of these informal agreements are reached between relatives or kin so ensuring that the girls receive a good education and a good dowry. Many childless couples adopt in this way. It is not unusual for maternal or paternal aunts to bring up one of their own siblings' children without going through any legal formalities. Children in these arrangements are often seen as *zamanats* (gifts which need to be returned at a later stage). The commitment taken on by adoptive parents have serious implications. Arranging a marriage, providing a dowry and generally providing a child with a good education are all part of these commitments. Boys are seldom given up for informal or formal adoption, except in cases where a parent has died and the surviving parent is unable to provide for him. It is not known how many children from Asian backgrounds are the subject of these arrangements in Britain.

Delegating the care of children through fostering and informal adoptions is known to be fairly common in Afro-Caribbean, and especially West African societies. Holman (1975) makes a distinction between what he calls 'exclusive fostering' and 'inclusive fostering'. Exclusive fostering attempts to contain the foster child within the foster family while severing past connections. Inclusive fostering is more open and promotes a variety of familial and caring relationships. Inclusive fostering and a fluidity of family relationships is said to be especially characteristic of West African culture. Yet the nature of such fostering arrangements is often misunderstood in Britain. For example, in the 1950s a significant number of mature Nigerian students came to Britain with their children. Finding it impossible to obtain family accommodation, they resorted to private fostering arrangements. This led to charges that these parents did not care about their children. In many West African countries, however, it is not unusual for women to live independently of their husbands and it is also generally the case that children are made welcome in other households. Ellis (1971) notes that children in West Africa are often to be found living away from their parents and are sent to stay with relatives or friends for a variety of reasons that would not be thought to warrant fostering in Britain. Such children may be visited infrequently by their parents. Ellis argues, however, that this does not mean that the parents do not care for their children's welfare but, on the contrary, if the child is being cared for by grandparents, a relation or even a co-wife, the mother may not wish to give the impression that she is spying to see how the children are being reared. Here is a notion of parental responsibility quite alien to western European thinking.

The significance of parental failure

Returning to the Bangladeshi families in my own study, one of the things I observed was that feelings of guilt about parental failure and tendencies to victim blaming were common. If a child grew up to conform to the cultural and religious beliefs of the society, it would be seen as a shining example for the family and much admiration for the father would ensue. If a child deviated from the norm, the mother would always get the blame for this, never the father. This tendency could be taken so far that a mother's relatives and ancestors would be blamed for her child's misdemeanours. Explanations would be sought in terms of who on the mother's side of the family was to blame for a child's deficiencies. Sometimes the search for a scapegoat would go back several generations so as to identify which of the mother's female forebears could have transferred her 'bad blood' to the child. As we have seen, it was mothers and sometimes maternal grandmothers who reared and cared for children, and when it came to apportioning blame and seeking explanations for a 'faulty child', it was they who would carry the brunt of criticism. The father's family and paternal grandmother would often claim that, if only they had cared for the child, their positive influence would have avoided such misfortune.

To illustrate, in one of the families studied, a child was suffering from a bout of measles. The child had not been fully immunised because of the father's strong religious objections. This father explained to me why the child had measles: '.... its not because he has not had all his injections, but due to the fact that my wife cooked meat in the house when I strictly forbade her to do so because of our neighbour's child having measles'. It transpired that when the neighbour's child had measles it had been brought to this man for advice because he was respected for his religious knowledge. This had infected his own child. In accordance with religious codes and cultural norms, he instructed his wife not to cook meat in the house for seven days since this represented a cleansing period. Because she had not observed this injunction, the mother was blamed for the child's suffering.

It is hardly surprising in this strongly patriarchal culture that praise and blame should be apportioned in this way. What is just as significant, however, is the moral significance of praise and blame.

The perceived failure of a child, even when attributable to congenital abnormality, represented a failure of parenting. In a culture in which family, kinship and community support was vital, people were anxious that they should not be seen by their failure as parents to have let their wider family or community down.

The provision of services

Given the cultural specificity of family life and differences in expectations and beliefs about the nature of parental responsibility, just how do services for children such as those in Luton's Bangladeshi community work? I shall consider three aspects of this question: first, the problems which arise because of tensions between, on the one hand, traditional practices and beliefs and, on the other hand, the scientific 'wisdom' of health and social care professionals; second, the ways in which services may sometimes be resented as an encroachment on family life; third, the accessibility of services to minority communities of this nature.

Traditional belief vs. scientific 'wisdom'

Conflict between Bangladeshi families and service providers tended to focus around four kinds of tradition: traditions of explanation; traditions of ritual; traditions of diet; and traditions of discipline.

Perceptions of and explanations for disability or learning difficulty were very specifically culture bound. Service providers tended to assume that the relatively high incidence of learning disability in the Luton Bangladeshi community might have a genetic cause and that consanguineous marriages or cousin marriages were to blame. However, the Bangladeshis disputed this. Their explanations were dependent in part upon the folklore and mythology of their culture. Both 'externalising' and 'internalising' factors were blamed. Young (1983) has argued that these two different kinds of belief help people explain the aetiology and the nature of an affliction. On the one hand, externalising belief systems attribute sickness or disability to pathogenic agencies which are often human or anthropomorphised. Explanations for affliction may focus upon the events which brought the victim to the attention of the pathogenic agency, such as grudges which may have been revenged through witchcraft, or lapses in ritual observance which may have been punished by ancestral spirits. Internalising belief systems in contrast are more compatible with physiological explanations. Physiological explanations may be rationalised in a pragmatic context by a particular theory or set of theories.

The Bangladeshi families believed by and large that their children's afflictions had arisen outside their children's bodies and could be linked to past events. None the less, they also accepted that internalising factors had a role to play. As there is no Bengali word to explain learning difficulties, their children were often labelled as 'mad' (*paagal*). The stigma of madness in their community was such that the children were then highly protected from the outside world. It was assumed that if the child was hidden away and pressurised into performing everyday skills like feeding, dressing and washing themselves, people would eventually accept them as normal and 'no one would ever know'. One sixteen year old boy explained that his parents were arranging a marriage for him and that getting married would cure him of the 'evil eye' that had been affecting his life. It was assumed that his wife would look after him when his own parents and siblings may not be able to undertake these tasks. This boy was severely physically handicapped and in a wheel chair with the mental age of a seven year old.

One of the traditional rituals to cause concern amongst health professionals is the use of *surma* . Aslam and Healy (1989), describe this ritual in great detail. Studies in Britain indicate that the practice of applying *surma* to the eyes of children can be damaging. If it is used over a long period it can, because of its high lead content, cause blindness and other ophthalmic conditions in later life. Health Visitors and other health care professionals have been actively discouraging this practice and attempts have been made to have the product banned from Britain. The practice flourishes none the less amongst the Luton Bangladeshis as an integral part of child-rearing practices. It fulfils two functions. First, it is thought to strengthen the eyesight. One father explained - '*surma* improves the eyesight so that even a child can thread a needle in the dark'. Secondly, the black *surma* has powerful symbolic significance, warding off evil spirits or *nazar* externally, and countering diseases internally. The full significance of this ancient ritual did not seem to be appreciated by health workers. Though children with learning difficulties were regarded very much as 'children of a lesser God', it was important to parents to protect them from evil spirits who may inflict further damage: these children were innocent and could not be corrupted if there was a symbolic black token painted on their bodies.

A practice in some ways comparable to that of 'doing the month' (as described in relation to Chinese women - see Pillsbury 1978) is also a common ritual feature among the many cultural groups of the sub-continent of India and Pakistan. Following the birth of a child women are required for a prescribed period to conform to cultural rituals bearing upon the care of the new baby. The rituals are thought to protect the child from evil spirits and harmful agencies. Apart from the rituals required of the mother, the new born baby is not bathed until the seventh day when the hair is shaved from its head and, in the case of the male infant, the religious ritual of circumcision is performed by the Imam or religious leader, rather than a qualified medical doctor. Aspects of these rituals offend western concepts of hygiene and safety.

Turning to questions of diet, in keeping with the traditions of the sub-continent and Middle Eastern cultures, sugar played a very important role in the diets of Luton's Bengali children. Weaning was often not attempted until the child was at least eighteen months old. Until this time the child's diet would consist principally of cows milk with high doses of sugar added to it. Other drinks with a high sugar content were also popular. This diet would sometimes be supplemented with toast and butter, topped with sugar. This often resulted in anaemia and vitamin deficiency. Dental health could also be a problem because of the high sugar diet. However dental care for Bangladeshi children has improved with the appointment of dentists from the Asian communities. It was interesting that, as a result of messages from health professionals about the general hazards of sugar, the thread worms, hookworms and tapeworms which infest the children who have been born abroad or have had frequent visits to their parents' country of origin were sometimes blamed by parents on the quantities of sugar in their diet.

Ghee (clarified butter), was another popular food which is given to children as a topping on chappati or roti with sugar added to it. This would be broken into small pieces (*khachoori*), and fed during weaning. *Ghee* and sugar play a very significant role in weaning practices. From different religious viewpoints, *ghee* is the food of the gods in Hinduism, and a strength giving food for Muslims. *Ghee* and honey may have significance at the birth of a child in both Muslim and Hindu households. In Islamic households, after the first prayer in the ear of a newborn child (*azaan*) the baby is offered a piece of cloth or finger dipped in *ghee* and honey to suck. This practice is important as babies are not offered breast milk until the colestrum has disappeared from the mother's milk. Health professionals, of course, are concerned that babies are denied the more essential nutrients which the colestrum contains.

The significance of food within the child rearing practices of different cultures has been more widely discussed elsewhere (see, for example, Helman 1990; Aslam and Healy 1981; Kleinman 1980).

Asian cultures of course differ in their caring and rearing of children from Afro-Caribbean and African cultures. We have already discussed the fostering practices of some African cultures. There is evidence that many Nigerian parents believe that, if they are lenient in training their children, they will bring misfortune to themselves and their children. According to folk and traditional beliefs the child is born 'imperfect' and, if given its own way, will end up being foolish and do harmful things not only to him or herself but to other people as well. Parents therefore believe it is their duty to curb the evil nature of their children (Hake 1972). Discipline plays a very vital role in the rearing and caring of Nigerian children.

In this, Nigerian parents are actually not so different from Bangladeshi parents in inflicting a traditional upbringing and stern principles upon their children. In many of these cultures the children are expected to learn by observing and listening. Respect for elders is instilled at a very early age. It is difficult to make comparisons of child rearing practices between one culture and another. A beating to chastise a child in one culture might be perceived as traumatic for the child, but in another culture may project an expression of proper parental concern. In my own study with Bangladeshi families one father explained: 'My other two boys were slow as well and every one said that they were mentally backward, and that I should not discipline them with the occasional smack. But look at them now. They are both doing well at school and there is no evidence that they were slow or retarded. They were just lazy'. This statement was made after the youngest child in the family had been diagnosed as having severe physical and mental handicaps. The father was convinced that, with some discipline, his youngest son would perform as well as his other two.

However, traditional child rearing practices may be inhibited by fear of professional or legal intervention. For example, the exercise of discipline may be moderated for fear of prosecution for child abuse, or of the removal of children by the authorities. This is a particular concern within Asian communities and kinship networks will often come to the aid of parents rather then involving the authorities. This may explain the relatively small numbers of Asian children being looked after by local authorities and the evident reluctance of Asian communities to seek help and advise.

In some Asian cultures the misbehaviour of children may be blamed on the child's 'possession' by an evil spirit or *jhinn* (an affliction which is supposedly more likely to affect girls than boys). In recent years the British press and media have seized on instances in which parents or religious leaders have engaged in the 'exorcism' of *jhinns*. There have been cases in which girls have been beaten to death in attempts to rid their bodies of evil spirits. There have also been well publicised instances in which Asian fathers have beaten their daughters merely for disobedience. It is particularly important to Asian families that young girls should be kept 'pure' pending their eventual marriage. What welfare state professionals may regard as patriarchal brutality, may represent a part of the basic fabric of life within a particular ethnic community.

Service as encroachment

Amongst the Luton Bangladeshis, it was not unusual for mothers to take their children to the day care centres and wait outside all day for the time to collect their children and bring them back home. One day care centre had learned this fairly quickly and made provisions for the mothers to stay all day with their children. The staff could not bear to see the mothers waiting outside in the cold with no food or drink, wearing traditional clothes which did not protect them from the elements. The health, education and social services provided for Bangladeshi children with learning disabilities could be resented by parents if decisions were imposed on them without consultation. The exclusion of parents' views from the decision making process and the failure of service providers to explain their interventions contributed to the non co-operative attitudes of the parents. Parents were then labelled as difficult, especially when they demanded things which were thought by service providers to be 'trivial' rather than 'useful'. Sometimes there was little sympathy for the ways in which the Bangladeshi families needed to incorporate their religious, cultural and folklore beliefs into the way they conducted their lives.

However, such obstacles could be overcome. One mother had been repeatedly asked to attend a local health clinic with her nineteen month old daughter who had been born with a dislocated hip. The mother had failed to keep appointments for developmental tests because she did not feel the need to subject her daughter to them. She feared the tests would include 'manipulation' of the legs and cause her daughter suffering. Instead she had sought help from an elder female member of the community. The 'Healer' had advised massage of the child's legs with rape seed oil and to tie both legs together at night. A visit by the Health Visitor together with a linkworker resolved the impasse. A compromise was reached by which the mother could still massage her daughter's legs but seek physiotherapy from the local hospital.

Access to services

Athwall (1990) has noted that very little research has been undertaken into the needs of people with learning difficulties from many ethnic backgrounds, especially from within Asian communities in Britain. The Bangladeshis are in many ways the least recognised group within this category. This was certainly true of the Bangladeshis living in Luton and Bedfordshire. In spite of more recent attempts to address these issues, Bangladeshis still experienced difficulties of access to services. The capacity of parents to care for their children and fulfil their parental responsibilities could be restricted by language barriers and by lack of knowledge about local services and the respite care facilities that were available. More fundamentally, there was a deep rooted suspicion that if children were to receive these services, the agencies concerned would suspect that the parents could not cope with their children and may take them away, bringing shame on the parents and their community.

The majority of the first generation carers of children were women, a high proportion of whom were illiterate. They were unable to read or write English, Bengali or the Sylheti dialect leading to double discrimination by the service providers. This added to the isolation of carers and children alike. When help was needed in the rearing of children or with routine advice on health and education issues, the tendency would be for mothers to seek help among their own networks and community. Although support and advice was available in the majority of the health clinics on immunisation, weaning, respite care, nursery provision and special pre-school centres, there was evidence that these facilities were not utilised to their full capacity because parents assumed that the children would not be provided with religiously or culturally acceptable diets.

Parents from Bangladeshi backgrounds often lost out on help and support and, as a result children with severe learning difficulties were cared for primarily by mothers and sisters within the home with little intervention by outside agencies. Though carers often reported their anxieties and anger to service providers, they were seldom able to communicate effectively because of language difficulties. This had the effect of discouraging parents from keeping appointments and so undermined health promotion initiatives. Such initiatives were often painstakingly explained in leaflets published in local ethnic dialects, but the leaflets were only available in clinics.

Conclusions

In a multi-cultural society an assortment of expectations about child-rearing practices jostle, compete and sometimes conflict with each other. This must not cloud our judgement that public authorities and other caring agencies need as far as possible to protect children from harm. The issue, however, is far from easy.

We have seen that guidance to the Children Act of 1989 calls for information to be made available about cultural differences in parenting patterns. Modood, however, has spoken not merely about the need for information, but the need for relevant professionals to be trained 'in the complex character of racial inequality and difference, and in the appropriate cultural backgrounds'. He also calls for '

> the recruitment, training, and promotion of individuals who can positively relate to one or more of the marginalised minority groups and can infuse their understanding into the policy-making and implementation process' (1994: 16).

The evidence outlined above I believe supports that conclusion. Information about the cultural practices of ethnic communities is too complex to be passively assimilated and needs to be the subject of active training. What is more, where for example professionals may confront suspected child abuse, they must be equipped to understand, to evaluate, and if necessary to challenge assertions that acts were perpetrated for the good of the child or in accordance with legitimate custom. If services are to be rendered properly accessible and comprehensible to ethnic communities, it is essential that there should be mechanisms in place to ensure that the practitioners working with families have, not just information, but sensitivity towards the religious and cultural backgrounds of those families. To this end, it is increasingly important to employ people with the same cultural and religious backgrounds as the population they serve. Such professionals should act, not so much as ambassadors for their profession, but as ambassadors for the people of the ethnic communities, interpreting the ways in which welfare provision can be adapted to benefit children while fitting in with cultural traditions.

Modood has also argued that we should allow ethnic communities to use their traditions and values to meet their own problems and disadvantages. Upon the one hand, communities should be involved as partners at the level of strategic planning of services for children. Upon the other, we need to support and harness some of the 'wisdom' embodied in ethnic communities' own child-rearing practices. Certain intractable dilemmas will undoubtedly remain. However, policy makers and service providers must beware of substituting new and subtle forms of coercion for crude professional imperialism. Child-rearing may be one vehicle by which to pass on traditions and for keeping minority cultures alive.

I am grateful to Pat Ellis for helpful comments upon an earlier draft of this chapter.

6 'Burdensome' parents:
Reciprocity, rationing and needs assessment

Kathryn Ellis

The basis of family care

Relatives play a primary role in supporting older people who require practical help and personal care through illness or disability. Most of that care is provided by spouses, or others living in the same household, but adult children play a significant role in supporting parents living alone (Evandrou *et al* 1989). Changes in the age structure of the population over the twentieth century have led to rising numbers of older people, particularly the very old (Kiernan and Wicks 1990). The incidence of disability increases with age and, attached to severe levels of disability, there is a requirement for assistance with domestic and/or personal care (Johnson and Falkingham 1992). Demand has been heightened by the increased number of older people living in independent households (Johnson and Falkingham *op cit*), although Finch draws on empirical studies to suggest that Asian and African-Caribbean elders are three times as likely as white elders to live with relatives (1989b).

There is a tension between the growing numbers of older people wanting to live at home and the declining availability of family care-givers. Smaller families mean fewer children to provide care for older parents (Allen *et al* 1992), with one third of older people having no surviving children (Rimmer and Wicks 1983). If the immediate family is the only reliable source of consistent support of the family, families are also taking on increasingly diverse forms (Finch *op cit*). With most care of older relatives undertaken by women, increased economic activity amongst married women puts a further strain on the shrinking pool of available care-givers (Kiernan and Wicks 1990), as does increased mobility (Henwood 1992).

This issue of the match between demographic, social and economic change and government policy on community care will be examined shortly. Another important consideration, however, is the assumptions underlying policy interventions about the basis on which family care is provided. The consensus within the body of literature on family care is that members of the same kinship network are motivated to support each other in times of need first and foremost by feelings of duty. That sense of responsibility is more or less strong according to the particular kin relationship in which relatives stand to the person in need. In the white community, the parent-child relationship is positioned second only to the marriage relationship in a 'hierarchy of kinship obligations' (Qureshi and Walker 1989). Powerful cultural norms underwrite the duties to attach to this relationship such that it is widely seen as legitimate for parents to call on adult children in times of need. Insofar as decisions about caring are taken with regard for 'the proper thing to do', reflectively, adult children will seek to align their actions with public expectations (Finch and Mason 1990).

As indicated, the choice of care-giver is also gendered. Secondary analysis of the 1985 General Household Survey (OPCS 1987) revealed that, although men play a significant role in spouse care, women are still the primary providers of personal and practical care to older people (Arber and Ginn 1991). Consequently, daughters are preferred in respect of the provision of this type of assistance, and men are also able to discharge their caring obligations towards their parents through their wives, although sons may retain their traditional responsibility for economic support. Within Asian communities, sons are expected to be the main supportive bond for parents but, in terms of personal and practical care, that duty is also likely to be discharged through female relatives.

The issue of women's caring role within the extended family was taken up by feminists in the late 1970s as an extension of their interest in women's dominant role in child care (see Finch and Groves 1980; Equal Opportunities Commission 1980). From a materialist perspective, the identification of women as carers is embedded in the patriarchal relations of Western capitalism in which the male 'breadwinner' occupies a dominant role in both public and private domains by virtue of his engagement in the 'real' world of work carried out for profit whilst the 'housewife's' primary association with the private domain means her domestic and caring labour has remained invisible and unaccounted for. The reproduction of a patriarchal division of labour within the paid workforce leaves women subordinate in both spheres and vulnerable to poverty at every stage of the life-cycle (Glendinning and Millar 1992). As Graham (1983) points out, the dominant division of labour creates a socially constructed dependency for women that, paradoxically, is founded on the dependence of others upon them for care.

The emphasis in early studies therefore was on making visible the extent to which intergenerational care by women should properly be regarded as work, with a cataloguing of the long hours and arduous physical and emotional labour frequently involved (Nissel and Bonnerjea 1982; Glendinning 1983; 1985). To explain how patriarchal relations are held in place, feminists drew on the work of writers such as Chodorow (1978) and Gilligan (1982) to conclude that women's behaviour was shaped by a different moral code to men, their identity as care-givers rooted in feminine values which predisposed them to privilege care of others over care of self. Graham (*op cit*) argued that women experienced these two different aspects of caring as one - the physical tasks of caring, or the 'caring for', being inseparable from the 'caring about', or feelings of love and concern for the recipient of their care. Because women were 'naturally' disposed to feel a commitment to both the relationship and activity of caring, they both expected of themselves and were expected by others to take on responsibility for personal care tasks. Ungerson (1981; 1987) suggested cultural taboos around cross-gender caring of an intimate nature reinforced the extent to which women's self-identity was closely associated with and lived out through the experience of providing care. Insofar as this type of caring is more closely proscribed for men than for women so it is strongly identified as 'women's work'.

But feminist accounts of 'informal' care developed in the early 80s have recently been subject to important critiques challenging assumptions of a unitary experience of oppression for women in the West. Williams (1989) and Graham (1991; 1993b), for example, draw on black feminist writings to point out that, although white middle class women's experiences of caring have hitherto been used as an implicit norm, the differential position occupied by black and working class women under a racialised and patriarchal capitalism means they experience 'family' and caring differently. Whilst these theoretical developments have yet to feed fully through into empirical studies of caring, of particular interest to this discussion are studies which are beginning to emerge examining 'informal' care from the perspective of the person cared for rather than the care-giver (Begum 1990; Morris 1993a).

The higher incidence of ill-health and disability amongst women, particularly those living alone, coupled with their greater longevity, mean that the primary recipients of care are older women (Arber and Ginn 1991; Hughes and Mtezuka 1992). Yet Morris (1991) argues that non-disabled feminists have tended to focus on the carer, marginalising the experiences and interests of people receiving care. As a group, older and disabled people are disadvantaged by a socially constructed dependency, created not by physical or mental incapacity, but in their lack of access to the means of independent living - particularly, though not exclusively, an adequate income (Walker 1980; Oliver 1990). Black and white working class women are most likely to be economically dependent in later life, having limited access to private pension provision and the experience of low income and poverty throughout life; they are also most likely to live in poor housing conditions (Hughes & Mtezuka, *op cit*). Older women receiving care are further disadvantaged because they have lost their primary identity as care-givers and have been forced into dependency on the care of other women - as unpaid 'informal' carers and/or low paid workers employed within community care organisations. Their treatment by non-disabled feminists as 'other' and as leading less valuable lives serves only to reinforce their oppression (Begum 1992; Keith 1992; Morris 1992).

What these latter critiques point to is the importance of interdependence in human relationships. Finch identifies the principle of reciprocity as a separate but linked concept to that of kinship obligations in the provision of family support (1989b: 167). When viewed as simple exchange, the principle is straightforward - support should be two-way with neither party receiving more than she or he gives. Yet, as Twigg and Atkin argue, the very concept of caring involves the performance of tasks of a supportive nature beyond the normal reciprocities common between adults (1994: 8). Because the exigencies of caring routines reduces the space for negotiation between the parties concerned (Ellis 1993), mutuality may be difficult to achieve where intensive support is provided.

However, in the case of parents and children, a longer-term view of the nature of reciprocity may be taken. Taking into account care provided to children when dependent, and financial and other types of assistance supplied over the parents' lifetime and after death through inheritance, parents are generally net givers of assistance to their children. Consequently, children owe a permanent debt of gratitude to their parents which they may only fully repay through the care and support they provide their own children (Finch *op cit*). Certainly Qureshi and Walker (1989) found this sense of reciprocity was strongly expressed by children as part of their motivation for caring. Given the culturally-defined asymmetry of the parent-child relationship, however, it is socially acceptable for children calculating whether and at what level to support parents to take their own material interests into account - although these may weigh less heavily in decisions to provide personal care than other forms of assistance (Finch *op cit*). Similarly, to the extent that caring is 'compulsory altruism' (Land and Rose 1985) for daughters in a way it is not for sons - at least for white, middle class women - calculations based on self-interest may be at odds with their identity as people who deny themselves for the sake of others.

The principle of reciprocity is also important for older people in ensuring they retain a sense of autonomy in family relationships. Given older people expect to be net givers throughout their lifetime, feelings of dependency may build up if they cannot reciprocate children's help. Where the caring relationship is not held together by mutual affection, only a sense of duty on the part of the care-giver may remain (Ungerson 1983). Particular problems are therefore posed for parents requiring intensive support who lack the emotional or material resources to reciprocate. Wilson argues that in these circumstances older people relying on children for care may ration their demands or have them rationed by their children (1993). At the same time, though, the concept of dependency may itself be gendered. Qureshi and Walker (*op cit*) found older men assumed daughters would care for them if their wives could not, the view that children are reciprocating for care received in the past being particularly pronounced amongst older men. Whereas patriarchal social relations may prevent men from feeling dependent even when receiving care, Keith suggests that women's primary identity as care-givers means they expect to be givers rather than recipients of care (1992).

Kinship obligations are clearly central to an understanding of why sons and daughters care for parents. Yet Finch emphasises the extent to which they should be regarded as 'normative guidelines' rather than a deterministic set of rules (1989b). Not only are gender, class, race, age and disability important mediating factors but so too are the history and quality of the interpersonal relationship. Pragmatic considerations, such as geographical distance, and other kin commitments, such as the care of children, also weigh in the calculations sons and daughters make about what support is required by parents and who can provide it (Qureshi and Walker 1989; Finch and Mason 1990; G.Parker 1991).

Community care - constructing relations between state, individual and family

From the mid-70s public expenditure control has dominated the social welfare agenda in Britain, and the influence of 'New Right' ideology on successive Conservative governments elected since 1979 has meant further fiscal restraint.

Expenditure controls have been legitimated in terms of 'possessive individualism' (Dalley 1988): rather than be forcibly dispossessed through taxation to finance the welfare of others, people have been encouraged to take responsibility for their own welfare. Although the welfare state was founded on the notion of providing for people in 'states of dependency' (Titmuss 1963), the expectation has been that older people will become increasingly self-sufficient. The virtues of self-reliance have been negotiated through discourses of active citizenship in which citizenship no longer stands for the right to welfare but the duty to make personal provision against the dependencies of disability and old age. At the same time, dependency on the state has been discouraged by deterring people from using services - or, at least, providing only the bare minimum. As Rees argues, to be economically inefficient, and therefore dependent on welfare provision, is no longer morally justifiable (1991: 51-2).

Accordingly, Warnes (1993) points out that older people have been represented as a social and economic burden on the working population, particularly in respect of the financing of state pensions. Yet the precise relevance of growing numbers of older people to health and social costs is open to debate (Gibbs 1991; Taylor-Gooby 1991). The 'demographic burden' thesis also fails to take account of the extent to which, if only in economic terms of intergenerational transfers of wealth, older people are actually net contributors. Its true significance is arguably as a rhetorical device for justifying the reduction of expenditure on public support services and persuading the family to take on greater responsibility for the care of older people. At the same time, older people have been represented by policy-makers as an increasingly affluent group for whom rising levels of home ownership and occupational pensions mean an increased ability to take personal responsibility for their welfare - despite evidence that the state remains the dominant source of income for most people over retirement age, particularly women (Gibbs *op cit* ; Johnson and Falkingham 1992). Falkingham and Victor (1991) argue that whereas older people have traditionally been exempt from spending cuts, the myth of the 'Woopie' (well-off older person) helps legitimate increased charges for and selectivity in public services, including the personal social services.

Independence is the preferred option in respect of community care services: 'formal intervention should be kept to the minimum necessary in the interests of all concerned' (SSI 1991: 62). But, as Brown and Smith point out, personal responsibility is more difficult to insist on where people are experiencing old age, physical frailty, learning disability or long-term mental distress and 'cannot easily be construed as making an individual choice in eschewing independence and self-sufficiency' (1993: 186). Where individual liability cannot be enforced, the 'family' has a duty to take over. Finch (1989b) points out that, despite massive demographic, economic and social change, the presumption underlying British social policy is still of the 'naturalness' of family feeling - although, paradoxically, the state has long found it necessary, whether directly or indirectly, to persuade families to discharge their moral obligation to provide care.

As an example of direct persuasion, Finch (*ibid*) draws attention to the principle of the 'liable relative' embodied in the 1834 Poor Law (Amendment) Act according to which sons were made financially responsible for costs incurred by the parish in providing care for their parents. The current requirement for close relatives including children to underwrite or top up residential care fees on behalf of older family members, or pay the costs of domiciliary services, may be seen as a contemporary reworking of the principle of the 'liable relative'. Yet, to the extent that Victorian legislation persuaded families to 'lose touch' with older parents (Finch *ibid*), enforcing financial liability may prove counter-productive - even linked perhaps to the practice dubbed by the media as 'granny dumping'. In denying parents the opportunity to transfer resources to children during their life-time or after death, the current practice of forcibly applying older people's capital assets to residential or domiciliary charges compromises the material interests identified earlier as a legitimate part of negotiations between parents and children around the provision of care. Hughes and Mtezuka (1992) point out that elders from the New Commonwealth and Pakistan are placed in a particularly dependent position by the undertaking relatives must sign under current immigration rules that there will be 'no recourse to public funds' in the matter of their welfare.

Finch (1989b) also highlights the way in which the introduction of the Household Means Test in the 1930s reinforced the financial liability of relatives by treating the whole household as an economic unit. This principle persists in contemporary income maintenance arrangements in respect of older and disabled people in the way in which benefits paid to the recipient of care act as 'passports' to carers' benefits. Calculating the contribution which should be made towards the cost of adaptations under Disabled Facilities Grant legislation on the basis of household income similarly disturbs the principle of reciprocity around which caring situations are negotiated. In a study of needs assessments, the author found that where, for example, older people were sharing a household with adult children, neither party felt it was just that the carer should be liable for any part of the cost of a stair-lift or ramp, particularly as such adaptations could potentially detract from the future value of the property (Ellis 1993).

Given the trend towards the maintenance of independent households amongst older people, the treatment of the household as an economic unit has only limited value in enforcing filial obligations. The development of community care policy since the late 1970s is more readily analysable in terms of the less direct means by which the state ensures the continuing provision of care by the family. In order to spread liability across households, the principle of the 'liable relative' has been operationalised largely through assumptions about the increased availability of family support implicit in the withdrawal or increasing selectivity of services.

The change in policy direction from the mid-1970s, commonly characterised as a shift from care in the community to care by the community (Bayley 1973), coincided with growing public expenditure restraint. In the 1960s and 1970s policies aimed at resettling, or keeping people out of, institutions formerly designated for those requiring long-term asylum may be seen, in part, as an attempt to redress an historic imbalance of funding within the National Health Service favouring acute care. The series of government documents identifying as 'priority groups' for expenditure the so-called 'Cinderella groups' requiring chronic care - people designated in the terminology of the time as mentally handicapped, mentally ill or elderly (DHSS 1971; 1975; 1978) - was consistent with the social democratic discourses of greater equity in which policy was inscribed. At the same time, Bamford (1990) argues that the publication of a white paper explicitly identifying priorities for spending and managing within existing budgets (DHSS 1976) may be seen as marking the end of a period of expansion over the 1970s in the development of domiciliary services to replace institutionally-based care.

Maria Evandrou and colleagues argue that the policy focus has changed since 1979 from an emphasis on priority groups, targets, and planning towards expenditure restraint as an end in itself and a shift in the balance of provision from the state to the non-statutory sectors (1991: 213). An echo of an appeal to the theme of 'care in the community' appeared in the 1986 Audit Commission report which criticised the perverse incentives for people to enter residential care created by the social security system. In seeking to change the basis of funding from a largely demand-led to a predominantly supply-led budget, however, the primary concern may be read as containing spending. The legislation eventually to emerge from government reviews of community care over the 1980s made community-based services still more discretionary. By tightly rationing health care, the NHS & Community Care Act 1990 has also had the effect of diverting demand from a universalist service free at the point of delivery to a highly selective service for which all but the poorest are charged.

However, the residualisation of the state sector has been negotiated primarily through the new 'mixed economy of welfare' promoted by the 1988 Griffiths review of community care. Under reforms, local authorities would no longer directly provide the majority of services but 'enable' the contribution of other care-providers, both formal and informal. The white paper 'Growing Older' published in 1981 had already signalled the extent to which the government expected shortfalls in state provision would be made up by informal supporters (Langan 1990; Dalley 1993) whilst the Griffiths report made clear that 'families, friends and neighbours and other local people' would 'continue to be the primary means by which people are enabled to live normal lives in community settings' (Griffiths 1988: para 3.2).

What might the match be between people's own expectations of public support for their household situations and the current policy agenda for community care? Given a choice, the evidence is that the family is the last rather than the first resort in terms of the preferred option of older people for support, particularly in respect of personal care (Finch 1989b; Finch and Mason 1990). Demand for services goes up as they become less targeted (Daatland 1990). Contrary to assumptions on the part of policy-makers that dependency on the state is damaging to people's self-esteem, parents are more likely to feel dependent as a result of being obliged to rely on children. Further, the principle of reciprocity underlies the model many older people have of their relationship to 'the welfare state'. Having insured themselves against the liabilities of dependency, older people feel they are entitled to its support when required. Nor, to the extent that kin relationships are negotiated rather than, as implied in policy discourse, governed by absolute duties and rights can family support be regarded as either 'natural' or inevitably forthcoming. As Cheetham (1993) points out, community care is highly 'political' involving as it does endemic conflicts of interest - the enforced dependency of many older people, the conflicts and strains of carers, mixed views about family and state responsibility, and the overwhelming excess of demand over supply.

Decentralisation and the rationing of community care

Since the mid-80s the policy emphasis in respect of social welfare has shifted from one of explicit withdrawal from the post-war welfare state to the restructuring of its institutions through a combination of marketisation and managerialism (Taylor-Gooby and Lawson 1993). The 1986 Audit Commission report on community care emphasised the need for social services departments to use resources more efficiently, a theme picked up by Sir Roy Griffiths when he was appointed by the Prime Minister to investigate its criticisms. The three 'E's' of neo-Taylorist managerialism - economy, efficiency and effectiveness - articulated with a government agenda of public expenditure restraint by promising to deliver better services for less money (Newman and Clarke 1994). However, the principles of 'new public management' underlying the restructuring of the public sector over the 80s also draw on the orthodoxies of 'new managerialism', a key feature of which is the decentralisation of policy administration to the periphery whilst tight control over strategy and resourcing is retained at the centre (Taylor-Gooby and Lawson *op cit* ; Clarke, Cochrane and McLaughlin 1994).

Although the periphery is charged with responsibility for defining the type of need for community care to which it will respond and the level at which that response will be made (Harding 1992), the promulgation of government policy through detailed guidance, centrally monitored by the Audit Commission and Social Services Inspectorate (SSI), has meant expectations about style of response have been increasingly shaped at the 'core' (Lawson 1993). Critically, the level of response local authorities may make to the needs of their local population has been tightly controlled through central government methods of financing. In effect, social services departments have been passed the responsibility for rationing. As central government guidance acknowledges 'local authorities .... have a responsibility to meet needs within the resources available and this will sometimes involve difficult decisions where it will be necessary to strike a balance between meeting the needs identified within available resources and meeting the care preferences of the individual' (DoH 1990: para. 3.25). Because local authorities lack a clear logic for their provision, there is a danger that the rationing of community care services will become an end in itself. Indeed Salter (1994) suggests that the NHS and Community Care Act has elevated the contingency of need on resources available to the level of public principle.

At the same time, rationing is opposed to the ideological framework of community care which promises greater flexibility and choice for consumers. At a policy level, the contradiction disappears within discourses of new managerialism and consumerism. On the one hand, each level of the decentralised organisation is assigned sufficient autonomy and flexibility to bridge the gap between supply and demand (Langan and Clarke 1994: 84) and, on the other, the marketplace of care is subject to the discipline of consumer sovereignty. Local authorities though have been left to bridge the gap between policy rhetoric and the reality of cash-limited budgets through the construction of increasingly tight eligibility criteria.

Need is identified by the SSI as 'the requirements of individuals to enable them to achieve, maintain or restore an acceptable level of social independence or quality of life, *as defined by the particular care agency or authority* ' (SSI, 1991: 12, emphasis added). Care agencies typically devise eligibility criteria in terms of a medical model of disability and ageing according to which need is defined narrowly as physical or psychological dependency. As Morris (1993b) points out somebody may 'need' help with housework but not qualify for assistance under strict eligibility criteria which rule out those not dependent enough. To the extent that needs become the categories created by senior managers and policy-makers to define them (Smith 1980), people's 'independence' is reduced exponentially in line with expenditure cuts. Older people with family support have also been discriminated against in the allocation of services (Finch 1989b; Qureshi and Walker 1989; Parker 1990), a pattern which is likely to be sharpened by budgetary regimes which require social services departments to target resources on those most in need, often defined as people without carers (Twigg and Atkin 1994). With the concept of 'independence' restricted to maintenance of a 'minimum quality of life' through the provision of physical care, older and disabled people are likely to become increasingly 'institutionalised' in their own homes or forced into dependence on the care of relatives (Morris 1993a).

Charging policies deepen people's dependency. Social care is already targeted on people who are economically dependent with 80 per cent of personal social services' users estimated to live at or near the poverty line (Becker 1991). Charging may well serve to deflect services from those most in need but least likely to be able to pay onto those in lesser need of care (Gibbs 1991). Stevenson and Parsloe (1993) argue that community care is squeezing the relationships and living arrangements of people requiring support for their household situation, progressively restricting their life-styles as they go without services. Greater choice and independence, the by-words of reforms, may actually be determined by ability to pay.

Changing the meaning of care

The introduction of market and managerialist principles into public care has not only acted as a form of rationing but has arguably altered its very meaning. From a feminist perspective, this change can usefully be explored in terms of the masculinisation of caring services. Here the ascendancy of 'masculine' values of rationality, efficiency and hierarchy within social services departments is underwritten by a patriarchal division of labour in which women have traditionally provided direct caring services under the control of male managers (Hanmer and Statham 1988; Dominelli and McLeod 1989; Hallett 1989; Baines, Evans and Neysmith 1991). Langan and Day argue that restructuring further concentrates power in the hands of a small group of largely male managers and accountants at the 'core' who exercise authority over a mass of largely female and increasingly deskilled care workers at the periphery (1992: 67).

Historically, as the 'caring professions' came under male leadership and management, the 'feminine' ethic of care comprising both 'caring for' and 'caring about' which governed styles of interaction between a predominantly female workforce and clientele was fractured by what Land (1991) terms a 'scientific rationality'. Here the instrumental is privileged over the expressive, and formally acquired expertise over informally acquired, intuitive knowledge and skills. Land argues that the subsequent introduction of an 'economic rationality' into the caring services has meant public care has come to be defined primarily in terms of its monetary value (*ibid*). Given the danger of treating care as a commodity is that its costs are made explicit, Brown and Smith (1993) argue that formal 'packages of care' contain public liability by limiting the time paid workers spend on caring and restricting its meaning to the discrete tasks of 'caring for'. The authors follow Hearn and Parkin (1987) in suggesting that the latter is a peculiarly masculine way of looking at the world: a male hierarchy distances itself from the less visible costs of 'caring about' - the moral obligation, the time involved, and the restrictions imposed - and relegates them to low-paid women carers and, beyond that, to the family whose commitment to caring can be assumed to be boundless.

This reductionist model of public care also reinforces traditional patterns of service allocation in which, on the one hand, the needs of the person cared for are defined narrowly in terms of physical or psychological dependency and, on the other, the care-giver is treated instrumentally as the means to reduce that dependency. Warnes (1993) argues that, by focusing on the physical tasks of 'caring for', the person receiving care is constructed as a 'burden' on the care-giver and the caring relationship reduced to who does what for the weaker party. As care is commodified so a price tag is attached to 'dependency' with the cost of care calculated in terms of the physical and mental 'burden' the impairments of the person cared for represent to the care-giver. Warnes suggests that 'dependency scales', developed in some areas as a way for contractors to cost the care provided in nursing homes, could come to apply to the assessment of the care needs of older people more generally (*op cit*).

The principle of reciprocity on which parent-offspring caring situations rest is disrupted first by allocating services according to familist ideologies which make parents dependent on liable relatives then by changing the meaning of care in ways which obscure both the emotional reciprocity of caring relationships and the extent to which older people receiving significant support are themselves contributing members of the family (Morris 1993a; Parker 1993; Stevenson and Parsloe 1993). Morris (*ibid*) argues that, unless the concept of care includes the 'caring about', it acquires the meaning of 'taking charge' and is potentially abusive. According to one estimate 500,000 older people are at risk of abuse from relatives (Eastman 1984 quoted in Dalley 1993), and that abuse may be physical or financial. In respect of the latter, a grim form of community care indeed is created where older people are prevented from opting for residential care to protect their children's inheritance (Marchant 1993). At the same time, the representation of older people as a 'burden' suggests they are the problem for which the solution is to support the carer. The emergence of policies of 'supporting the carer' reinforce older people's vulnerability by positioning carers as the 'deserving' in new versions of public morality (Twigg and Atkin 1994) and thereby denying the very possibility of abuse (Stevenson and Parsloe 1993).

Yet carers may not be so much supported as disciplined into new roles under emerging community care regimes. Twigg and Atkin (1994) suggest the service model which most closely determines the response of community care organisations to 'informal' care-givers is that of 'carer as a resource'. Here services are provided as a supplement to rather than a substitute for 'informal' care, and care-givers are incorporated into service interventions as if they constituted a free resource to the caring situation. Whilst government policy guidance represents the relationship between the 'informal' carer and caring agency as one of 'mutual support' and 'shared responsibility' (DoH 1990: para. 3.28), the SSI advises practitioners that preventative support to alleviate stress on the care-giver should be prioritised in circumstances where the independence of the person cared for can be maintained (SSI 1991). Such advice is consistent with an instrumental emphasis on carers as the most cost-effective means of supporting the person in receipt of care which Twigg and Atkin suggest underlies the 'carer as a resource' model (*op cit*).

Bond argues there are signs that agencies are seeking to 'professionalise' the input of informal carers (1992). Certainly in their study of carers Twigg and Atkin (*op cit*) found relatives were being offered training to enable them to carry out semi-medical caring tasks in line with increasingly restricted access to health care. Additionally, as services become more fragmented and routinised, so Land suggests the result is "less personal and comprehensive care requiring more patching and piecing together by the carer at home" (1991: 17). In this way, as Baldock and Ungerson (1991) point out, the role of provider and co-ordinator of care is passing from the public to the private care-giver. As a largely female task-force of unpaid carer-givers is brought under the aegis of a patriarchal commissioning agency, Bond (*op cit*) suggests we may be witnessing a shift in the model of service responses proposed by Twigg (1989) from 'carer as a resource' to 'carer as co-worker'. Here the primary carer is no longer undirectable and unaccountable but represents the central point of articulation between formal and informal sectors, and the objectivisation of the 'burdensome' parent in new constructions of care is complete.

Negotiating care through assessment

Twigg and Atkin (1994) distinguish between the practice of qualified and unqualified staff on the basis of professional training, and the issue of whether professional codes of ethics act as a buffer against 'economic rationality' has been much debated in the social work press. Seen to threaten the integrity of traditional styles of practice are the fragmentation and specialisation of organisational roles within decentralised structures. Critically, as the assessment and care management process is broken down and assigned to different workers, so social workers have less freedom to engage in the longer-term relationships they regard as central to the discovery of need and the development of an appropriate response. Unless practitioners have the authority to plan interventions and manage workloads professional values may be a relatively weak force in assessment practice. Whilst social workers have traditionally been able to 'choose' their clients (Blaxter 1980), and have therefore had greater discretionary space to line up practice with training, occupational therapists (OTs) working in social services departments have not and their assessment practice has been routinised accordingly.

Nor have social workers tended to 'choose' to work with older people. Most social work interventions have been carried out by untrained staff and have focused on the allocation of practical aids rather than therapeutic support (Hughes and Mtezuka 1992; Hugman 1994). The separation of direct service work from accountability for resources under new regimes threatens further to institutionalise ageism by perpetuating this view of work with older people as routine, prescribable and of lower status (Hugman *ibid*); and the task-centred nature of interventions in respect of parent-offspring situations reinforces constructions of care discussed in previous sections. On the one hand an assessment of physical or psychological dependency is converted into the need to be 'cared for' and, on the other, the care-giver is treated instrumentally as a means of reducing functional dependency. This narrow view of household arrangements can mean assessors failing to consider interpersonal aspects of the caring relationship. For example, the author found in her study of needs assessments that an intervention commonly made by OTs in one authority was to organise hoist training for carers. In one situation she observed this meant the obvious stress a daughter carer was under as a result of the level of care she was providing was simply screened out (Ellis 1993).

Assessment ideologies which treat carers predominantly as a 'resource' and the person cared for as the object of their physical tending offer little incentive to use assessment as a means of uncovering conflict, despite SSI guidance that separate assessments should be carried out where that possibility exists (SSI 1991: 16). Professional training sets social workers apart from other staff working within the ambit of community care in giving them an awareness of, and the skills to work with, the conflicts of interest and ambivalent feelings of love, dislike, duty, dependency which may characterise parent-offspring caring situations. In their study, for example, Twigg and Atkin (1994) found social workers who were prepared to challenge dominant expectations and support relatives who chose not to continue caring. Yet, as indicated, deskilling is likely to mean that assessment is increasingly carried out by untrained staff with relatively low levels of autonomy.

In such circumstances, pressures associated with implementation of the NHS and Community Care Act - ambiguous policy objectives, a chronic shortage of resources, high demand, and raised public expectations - may lead staff to act as 'street-level bureaucrats' (Lipsky 1980), a way of thinking about the practice of community care in which there has been renewed interest of late (Cheetham 1993; Ellis 1993; Twigg and Atkin 1994). Charged with meeting too many needs with too few resources, social services staff deal with the resulting 'cognitive dissonance' (Schorr 1992) by developing their own survival techniques to ration their time and other resources.

From this 'bottom-up' perspective on policy implementation, the belief that reforms place 'rationing decisions firmly where they should be - with politicians and senior managers' (Audit Commission 1992: 26) is open to challenge. Assessment is represented in policy documents as the 'cornerstone' of reformed community care services (DoH 1989, para 1.11), the means by which the consumer exercises sovereignty and individual preferences are translated into flexible responses. Yet, at the same time, 'assessment must remain rooted in an appreciation of the realities of service provision' (SSI 1991: 14). Inbuilt accountability controls, such as the incorporation of eligibility criteria into assessment pro-formas, are designed to align decision-making with 'core' targeting objectives. In one study of assessment practice, however, researchers found that staff virtually ignored official pro-formas as assessments were adapted to the exigencies of the work environment and needs matched to available services (Hudson 1993). In the author's study, although staff felt assessment pro-formas meant they were losing the capacity to respond in a 'human' way to the diversity of people's situations, in reality their interventions were often highly stereotypical: under the pressure of insufficient time and other resources, staff developed narrow repertoires of routinised responses which, over time, came to dominate their assessment practice (Ellis 1993). Under prevailing conditions of implementation, as Cheetham (1993) suggests, care managers are just as likely as their predecessors to develop routinised responses.

The culture of the work group has been identified as a key influence in shaping those routinised responses, particularly for untrained staff (Satyamurti 1981; Ellis 1993; Twigg and Atkin 1994). The assessment ideologies of home care organisers are of particular interest as they have developed under conditions which will become increasingly prevalent as budgets are devolved to the front-line. The author's research suggests the assessment practice of this occupational group is already in tune with new agendas. To the extent that 'need' would be routinely equated in assessment with number of home care hours affordable within a cash-limited budget, the process of commodification appeared already to be well-established. Staff believed their traditional skills at managing within a fixed budget particularly equipped them for care management; and, indeed, the pride one home care organiser felt at her skill of 'wrangling', or staying within budget by taking from one person to meet the needs of another, represents in microcosm what was described earlier as a feature of reforms more generally, the privileging of cost-efficiency as the end rather than the means of interventions (Ellis 1993).

Studies of discretionary decision-making within social services departments suggest that not only are occupational values important in shaping practice but so too are personal values and attitudes (Rees 1978; Satyamurti 1981; Ellis 1993; Twigg and Atkin 1994). Over twenty years ago, Smith and Harris (1972) pointed out the efficacy of moral judgements as a rationing device in needs assessments for discretionary services. Given the conflation in organisationally-defined need between an assessment of dependency and the requirement for services, the author's research suggests that the primary aim of assessment for staff operating under the pressure of scarce resources becomes to ensure people remain 'independent'. Because assessors attempt to target resources on the deserving, and a common measure of 'deservingness' is self-reliance, denial of access to a service becomes morally justifiable. Such attitudes may be compounded by ageist assumptions which narrow the space for older people to negotiate their own definitions of need (Ellis 1993).

Common sense assumptions about the availability of family support may be similarly instrumental in a climate of scarce resources. What a member of staff in the author's study referred to as the 'thin dividing line' between caring family and home care service had to be vigorously defended. A rationing device commonly used in assessment was described by home care organisers as ascertaining what relatives would provide before explaining what help was available - a procedure legitimated in terms of 'we don't want to take anything away from the family'. Within assessment ideologies such as these, the withdrawal of support by offspring is illegitimate. A daughter requesting a chemical toilet for her mother threatened to stop visiting her on being told this service was for those without informal support. This was construed by the OT assistant concerned as an attempt to 'blackmail' the department (Ellis 1993).

From a 'bottom-up' perspective on decision-making then the services required to support parent-offspring caring situations are not so much allocated according to rational principles as negotiated. Yet authority over the discretionary space within which need is identified and the appropriate response developed is held largely by staff who themselves operate within increasingly tight financial constraints. Where the assessor's definition of the caring situation is directed largely towards managing and limiting demand, discretion will tend to be exercised negatively - an imbalance exacerbated by the relative powerlessness of people being assessed. In the author's study few people had any knowledge of or sense of entitlement to a service, and people who did constituted a threat and were treated defensively by staff (Ellis 1993). To the extent that help-seeking behaviour is itself gendered, women may be particularly disadvantaged by the lack of space within which to articulate their needs. As recipients of care, Hughes and Mtezuka argue that women's lower social expectations make them readier to accept the restrictions attached to ageing and disability, and therefore more inclined to get on and make the best of things (1992: 225-6). Because women are unused to having their customary role as care-giver reversed, they also tend to believe in self-help before assistance from any other source (Ellis 1993).

Conclusion

Government spending on community care services has decreased in real terms since the mid-70s, despite a widening 'care gap'. Policy-makers have made clear that the shortfall is to be made good by greater self-sufficiency on the part of older people with the family stepping in to meet the needs of those unable to finance their own care. The sense of responsibility adult children feel towards parents requiring assistance resonates at least in part with assumptions about familial obligations on which policy and practice is constructed. Yet, despite the 'naturalness' of family feelings through which government expectations of greater care by the community have been negotiated, some coercion has nevertheless been assumed to be required to persuade sons and daughters to discharge their obligations towards their parents. Hitherto the principle of the 'liable relative' in British community care policy has been operationalised primarily through a lack of public alternatives to family care being made available. Because, as feminists have long pointed out, family care tends to mean care by women that liability has remained largely invisible; and policy and practice have had scant regard for the greater sense of responsibility daughters may feel towards parents in times of need nor indeed of the greater willingness of fathers to rely on female kin for support.

Whilst uncomfortable tensions can be safely negotiated in policy rhetoric, local authorities must manage the increasingly sharp contradiction between supply and demand by constructing eligibility criteria which, on the one hand, define need in terms of ever-higher levels of risk and dependency on others for physical care and, on the other, identify the primary care-giver as a family member. As care is commodified so there is an intensification of the tendency within local policy and practice to position the person cared for as a 'burden' on the care-giver whilst treating the family member as a resource at the disposal not only of the person cared for but, increasingly perhaps, of the commissioning agency. In the case of the parent-offspring relationship this asymmetry runs counter to the expected direction of intergenerational giving, and parents reliant on highly selective community care services are particularly vulnerable as they are likely to have few material resources with which to reciprocate the care of offspring.

In terms of front-line practice, professional deskilling and the fragmentation of organisational roles intensifies the impact of what is perhaps the key disciplinary measure introduced by community care reforms - described by Gray and Jenkins as the conversion of spenders into managers of resources (1993: 12). Through the creation of what Langan and Clarke term a 'budget culture', successive tiers of management are persuaded to 'own' budgets and the responsibilities attached to them (1994: 80). Whereas assessment for selective welfare services has traditionally served the dual and contradictory function of assessing need and testing eligibility, by making care managers directly responsible for the budgets within which needs-based assessments must be accommodated, this ambiguity is sharpened; and the greater the responsibility practitioners have for managing resources, the more conservative their assessments appear to be. The routinised, often covert, responses staff develop to household situations as 'street-level bureaucrats' further limits the space parents and offspring have to explore their differing, perhaps conflictual, needs and interests.

Finch argues that, because models of kin obligations in British family policy have changed little over time despite the very different economic, social and demographic circumstances to prevail, significant gaps may emerge between government expectations and people's own understandings of what is realistic and reasonable in their own circumstances (1989b: 135). Yet although a credibility gap may already have opened up between the objectives of community care expressed in policy rhetoric and the reality of highly selective services for families requiring support for their caring situations

(Harding 1992), the majority of those involved have few spare resources with which to struggle against official assessments. It is only perhaps if the principle of the liable relative continues to be enforced through the imposition of financial penalities on close relatives that challenges to public policy may be mounted by more economically and socially powerful groups, and protest be more vigorously articulated.

7 Constructing the 'private carer': Daughters of reform?

Di Thompson

The 1990 NHS and Community Care Act defines a private carer as an individual 'who is not employed to provide the care in question' (Section 46). This official recognition of private, voluntary, 'unpaid' informal carers represents an important shift in central government policy.

This shift has arisen as an outcome of a series of welfare reviews since the 1970s culminating in an increased separation between the role of the state and the role of the family within welfare provision. Consecutive Conservative governments, since the election of the Thatcher administration in 1979, have adopted the political philosophy of 'the rolling back of the state'. This entails the state increasingly moving towards adopting a residual role within welfare provision, while simultaneously advocating the personal responsibilities of the individual and the 'family' for the provision of care for vulnerable members of society.

The majority of such private informal carers are women caring for frail, elderly or disabled relatives, either in their own or their relative's home. Private caring, therefore, tends to take place within an existing familial relationship and impacts particularly on mothers and daughters and daughters-in-law.

This chapter focuses upon a feminist critique of the social construction of the private informal carer and is presented in three sections. The first will trace some historical and contemporary debates and critiques of the ideological and discursive processes underpinning the intersection of the state and the family. The second will present a critique of the social construction of carers within particular policies and reviews leading up to the introduction of the 1990 Act. The third will consider the findings of current empirical research into familial attitudes towards caring. All three sections address the issue of how daughters and daughters-in-law in particular are positioned within the social construction of private carers.

Historical and contemporary debates and critiques within social policy and feminist theory

Making women 'visible'

Elizabeth Wilson in an article entitled 'Women, the "Community" and the "Family"' states:

> the "community" is an ideological portmanteau word for a reactionary, conservative ideology that oppresses women by silently confining them to the private sphere without so much as ever mentioning them (Wilson 1982: 55).

The rise of Second Wave Feminism within the 1970s has had a seminal impact upon raising awareness of women's 'invisibility' within traditional mainstream social policy and the operation of an androcentric ideology which 'reflects male concerns, deals with male activity and male ambitions and is directed away from issues involving or of concern to women' (Thiele 1992: 16). Of particular relevance to the theme of this chapter is the feminist critique which has enabled the operation of the public/private dichotomy to become visible, as exemplified in Elizabeth Wilson's statement.

This critique argues that traditionally women have been constructed within social relations in a subordinate position; relating to the private realm of 'the family', reproduction, domesticity and dependency. This occurred as an outcome of the rise of industrialisation and modern capitalism. Men, on the other hand, have been constructed as belonging to the dominant public and civil world of capitalist productive labour relations. Women's positioning within capitalist social relations, therefore, is one of a gendered subordination under patriarchal and capitalist hegemony.

This gloss over the 'feminist critique', however, does not take into account the differing theoretical and epistemological perspectives within feminist debates and feminist theory. This is not the subject of this particular chapter, but it should be noted that 'there is no single feminist social policy, partly because there is no single feminist theory' (Pascall 1986: 19). Notably, however, many feminists within the last decade have argued for the recognition of the inter-related nature of the private and the public and the visibility of women in both arenas: 'Women's position in the public spheres of work and politics cannot be viewed in isolation from their role in the private sphere of home and family' (Dale & Foster 1986: 44).

In relation of the theme of this chapter, what are some of the crucial factors that feminist academics have made 'visible' in order to analyse women's subordination within the construction of social relations? The first has already been discussed, the recognition of the structured nature of gender relations. Three further interrelated constructs have been mentioned and will be considered briefly in more detail: the notions of 'reproduction' and 'dependency'; the construction of a specific form of 'familial ideology'; and the rise of the 'bourgeois family', upon which the latter is based.

The notions of 'reproduction' and 'dependency'

Gillian Pascall argues that 'If reproduction is the bedrock of private life, it is also a substantial concern in public life; indeed, social policies may well be seen as state intervention in the reproductive process' (Pascall 1986: 21). The social construction of a woman's place within social relations, particularly mothers, daughters and daughters-in-law, is therefore a site of ongoing political struggle. Domestic reproduction, seen as the fulfilment of a servicing, nurturing and caring role through the process of reproducing social relations, becomes the focal point of state intervention, particularly within the auspices of the welfare state.

An essential aspect of this view of reproduction however is a move away from biological determinism (where women are seen as natural carers and nurturers as a result of their biological sex) to an understanding in terms of material relations which are primarily socially constructed. This opens up opportunities to de-construct, analyse and offer possible explanations for women's subordination which encompass the possibility for change. Fiona Williams takes up this point and expresses the usefulness of a social constructionist framework:

> What emerges from these 'social constructionist' accounts is that even though biological sex differences exist, what is important is the way biology interacts with the social and material conditions of women's lives, and although some aspects of biology may, at present, be unchangeable, the social and material conditions can be changed and challenged (Williams 1989: 64).

Nonetheless, the effect of the splitting of production and reproduction between the public and the private has, feminists argue, created a situation where women have been placed in a position of dependency within the family. Historically, this has been a recurring theme within feminism, from the early nineteenth century first wave feminists and the development of second wave feminism in the 1970s, to feminism today. However, within first wave feminism; especially after the successful campaign for the vote, there was a growth in welfare feminism which embraced the prevailing ideology of dependency and motherhood. Such feminists campaigned for improved welfare conditions for mothers and their families. Other early feminists, however, such as Eleanor Rathbone, argued that social policy placed women in economically dependent positions within the family. And indeed one important aspect of contemporary feminist critiques of social policy is directed towards the assertion that 'social policy - far from alleviating this dependency - plays a large part in sustaining it' (Pascall 1986: 28). This is particularly pertinent to women as private informal carers.

Women as carers has been a main theme of feminist writing, covering such areas as the degree and extent of the caring role, the economic costs of caring, the emotional content of caring and the level of distribution between the state and women in the caring role. However, before proceeding to look at this, there is one further important concept to consider and that is the social construction in the nineteenth century of a 'familial ideology' through the notion of the Bourgeois Family.

'Familial ideology' - the bourgeois family

The period of the 1830s onwards marked the influence of the rising middle class, the bourgeoisie. This class, Dalley (1988) argues, were increasingly adopting a philosophy of 'possessive individualism' which incorporated notions such as:

> an independent centre of consciousness; the notion of the self and self-determination; of privacy and freedom from intrusion....the human essence is freedom from dependence on the will of others, and freedom is the function of possession (Dalley 1988: 28).

This concept is intimately tied up with, but not reducible to, the development of a particular form of familial ideology, where the family is constructed as both a regulatory institution and a haven for privacy where 'the autonomous proprietorial individual....is male' (*ibid.*). This bourgeois, middle class, family became nuclear in basis, comprising a male breadwinner who owned and regulated his wife and children and protected himself and his family from intrusion - particularly intrusion from the state. Familial ideology, therefore, is based on a patriarchal relationship. Diana Gittins takes up this point arguing:

> Implicit in the concept of the western family, then, is the notion of male - and specifically, paternal - dominance over others. Thus by definition the family has been an unequal institution premised on paternal authority and power...Patriarchy is thus both a gender and an age relationship, based on power, and is essential in understanding families (Gittins 1993: 35).

This social construction of the family based upon reproduction, dependency, structured gender differences and women's subordination which arose in the nineteenth century appears to have taken on a symbolic universal perspective, and is particularly pertinent to the series of anti-collectivist governments' social policies since the late 1970s .

However, in reality, Diana Gittins argues, there is no such thing as 'the family' which implies a static entity. Rather families and kinship structures have always retained a fluidity whilst containing some defining characteristics which we may regard as pertinent to the concept of a family. None the less, the power of the particular construction of the bourgeois family lies in its apparent universalism and classlessness as well as its ability to conjure up commonly held beliefs and ideals. In short, Diana Gittins concludes, these beliefs have constructed a '*strong symbol-system which is labelled as the family*' (Gittins 1993: 70) [original italics].

This ideological symbol-system of the bourgeois family is frequently called upon when society is undergoing change and turbulence. Since the late 1970s Britain has been experiencing the effects of economic recession, an increasing ageing population and demographic changes. There have also been marked changes in the structures of families, particularly the rise in one parent families and the development of re-constituted families following divorce and re-marriage.

These social changes have brought about a concern within mainstream social policy that the family is in a 'state of crisis' and becoming too dependent upon the intervention provided by the welfare state. These fears arise partly because of changing employment patterns where more women are now entering the public domain of work; one of the major employers of women, indeed, being the various institutions of the welfare state.

Recent research undertaken on women's pay and family income inequality indicates that the 'male breadwinner' family model is in rapid decline and that women's earning are an essential contribution towards keeping families out of poverty (Harkness, Machin and

Waldfogel 1994). The research also indicates that changes within female employment have brought about a more equalising effect upon the distribution of income within households, primarily where partners were in low income employment. However, female employment too is frequently insecure, part-time, low-paid temporary or casual.

As we have seen in Chapter 6, a feared consequence of the changing patterns of employment structures and the increase in the elderly population by governments of the Right is that this may result in a 'crisis in care' as well as in a 'crisis in the family'; resulting in a lack of women, particularly daughters and daughters-in-law being available to take on the caring role. However, whether in fact there has been a change within familial attitudes towards the caring role is something which will be taken up later in this chapter.

The caring relationship

The academic literature on caring has clearly identified that the majority of informal 'private' caring is carried out by women, particularly daughters and daughters-in-law. And, although recent findings from the General Household Survey have highlighted far larger number of male carers than had previously been recognised, they primarily fall into the category of 'spouse' carers, and so are not specifically the subject of this chapter.

Clare Ungerson in her book *Policy is Personal: Sex, Gender and Informal Care* produced life-cycle typologies of the male and female informal private carers she had interviewed. The male carers in the study cared for their spouses and all had taken on their caring roles late in their life-cycle, after retirement. In contrast the women who were caring for elderly relatives entered the life-cycle typology at variable stages.

> Caring for an elderly dependant is nevertheless unlike child care in one important respect. Children have only one mother; elderly people generally have more than one child or child-in-law. In other words, the network of obligations and pressures on mothers to care for their children is rather different from the comparable pressures on children to care for their parents or parents-in-law. Mothers are spotlighted. Children, and especially daughters and daughters-in-law, are simply lit; their position in their personal life cycle provides the stage backdrop (Ungerson 1987: 84).

Sons and sons-in-law do not appear even dimly lit within this framework of expectations or obligations. Within this structuring of gendered kinship relations it is only women who appear to be the 'appropriate people to combine caring with paid work and child care and to care for dependants of a different generation from themselves' (Ungerson 1987). Other researchers too have identified a gendered 'hierarchy' of expectation or obligation as to who should care for elderly relatives. Qureshi and Walker's (1989) research identified the following kinship hierarchy: Spouse, daughter, daughter-in-law, son, other relatives, non-relatives.

The caring relationship itself, however, is highly complex. Feminist academics have identified several key concepts upon which the caring relationship is based. These include a sense of love, duty, reciprocity, obligation and responsibility; what Hilary Graham has termed 'a labour of love' (Graham 1983). One particular aspect, the notion of 'caring about' and 'caring for', Gillian Dalley contends is constructed and experienced differently by men and by women. She argues that at an affective level there can be a distinction drawn between 'caring for' and 'caring about'.

Caring *for* involves personal tending (Parker 1981), - for example, the servicing and maintenance 'tasks' of caring, whereas caring *about* is linked with emotion and feelings about another person (Graham 1983). Within the role of motherhood, these two notions Dalley argues have been constructed as a unified and 'natural' whole; linking indissolubly biological reproduction and social reproduction as the 'normal' state of affairs. This social construction of motherhood, however, extends beyond the 'normal' state of affairs to the 'extra-normal':

> Just as the affective links which form at birth are tied into the mechanical links of servicing and maintenance in the case of healthy children, similarly, the same affective links in the case of disabled and chronically dependent family members get tied to the servicing and maintenance functions (Dalley 1988: 10).

For a woman to go 'against the grain' and disentangle these two notions would be to behave in a deviant manner, challenging the social construction which is being presented as a natural essential of woman/ motherhood. For men, however, the situation is different: caring for and caring about can, and indeed Dalley argues, is assumed to be separate. Men, she contends, can care about but not necessarily have to or be expected to care for, through undertaking a tending role. Rather, men will assume responsibility for care. This responsibility is normally perceived as financial support gained from their superior positioning and participation in the 'public' world of paid work. Therefore, the 'good son' is one who, typically, provides for his parents and/or other relatives financially (and supports his wife financially while she does the tending)' (*ibid:* 12).

One of the ways in which the successful unification of the concepts of caring for and caring about can be understood is by referring to the work of Land and Rose (1985) on altruism. They argue that 'whereas altruistic practices are structured into women's lives they are structured out of men's' (Land and Rose 1985: 93). Women, they contend, have internalised the values underpinning the concepts of caring for and caring about as presented within the ideological discourses of the nuclear family and the expectations and prescriptions of social policies. This process of internalisation has been termed 'compulsory altruism', a process which 'encapsulates both the self-sacrifice and the selflessness involved and the prescriptive expectations of society that women shall perform that role' (Dalley 1988: 17).

A further explanation of the social construction of the difference between men and women's 'positioning' in relation to the caring role explores the notion of internalisation through the concept of 'motherhood' and 'identity' from within a psychodynamic perspective. Chodorow argues that the caring role is deeply embedded in social structures to the degree that 'the sexual division of labour and women's responsibilities for child care are linked to and generate male dominance' (Chodorow 1978: 76). Mothering, therefore, reproduces itself and is experienced differently for boys and girls resulting in differential identity outcomes.

> I argue that the relationship to the mothers differs in systematic ways for boys and girls, beginning in the earliest period. The development of mothering in girls - and not in boys - results from differential object-relational experiences, and the ways these are internalized and organized. Development in the infantile period and particularly the emergence and resolution of the oedipus complex entail different psychological reactions, needs and experiences, which cut off or curtail relational possibilities for parenting in boys, and keep them open and extend them in girls. (Chodorow 1978, p91).

This argument maintains that through the process of the unconscious caring is 'given to women...while at the same time caring is taken away from men: not caring becomes a defining characteristic of manhood' (Graham 1983: 18). Feminine and masculine identities are formed within this dynamic. To transform such identities requires a transformation in reproduction away from the site of the family and where men can play an active role in the reproductive process.

Jane Lewis and Barbara Meredith in their research on daughters caring for mothers at home also identified a strong internal injunction to care among the daughters they interviewed. However, their findings temper the 'self-sacrificing' and 'selflessness' of compulsory altruism. This internal injunction was linked with a positive concept of female identity which could potentially be explained through Chodorow's notion of the internal construction of 'motherhood'. Equally, however, the same daughters also experienced strong 'external' pressures from the expectations of others; friends, neighbours and relatives, that they would fulfil the caring role.

The great majority of the carers they interviewed reported that they wanted to care and would do so again despite the emotional and material costs, the degree of labour required and the psychological adjustments to their elderly mothers' deteriorating condition; with the contingent changing quality of their personal relationships that that entailed. Their conclusions were:

> While caring should be seen as part of the construction of femininity, women do not necessarily experience caring as either a matter of self-sacrifice or of powerlessness. Positive feelings about caring are often derived not only from abstract satisfaction at obeying the injunction to care, but from the reality of the caring experience, and in particular from the companionship, emotional security and appreciation it brings the carer (Lewis and Meredith 1988: 153).

The caring relationship, therefore, is complex and often experienced in contradictory ways but most importantly, it combines what Hilary Graham describes as 'both the identity and the activity of women in Western society' (Graham 1983: 30).

Summary

The feminist social constructionist critique of the caring relationship argues that what women 'experience' as natural has in fact been socially constructed through the placing of reproduction within the private sphere of the family. Therefore, when daughters and daughters-in-law perceive, and experience, caring as a natural fulfilment of familial duties, or a willing repayment of their natural debt to their parents, or a natural expression of their feminine identity, they are interpreting and experiencing social constructions as essentially lived 'facts'. These 'facts', however, are not naturally or biologically given 'truths', but are powerful ideological constructs within a particular hegemonic patriarchal form of social production and reproduction. As such, therefore, they are open to challenge and possible change.

The next section outlines a feminist critique of the development of ideological constructs within recent community care policies. The section traces the shift in political emphasis for responsibility for welfare provision from the state to families as the first line of support. This will then be compared with the findings of recent empirical research on kinship relationships and responsibilities which is explored in the final section.

The emergence of community care in social policy and the government reviews leading up to the introduction of the 1990 NHS and Community Care Act

The emergence of community care

The construct of 'community care' rather like 'the family' is generally regarded as 'a good thing'. The actual origins of the discourse are obscure however. But within the post-war period there was growing concern at the high cost of maintaining large mental handicap and mental illness hospitals as well as the inhumane effect that such institutionalisation had on patients.

A policy was developed to close such institutions and transfer patients to smaller units 'in the community'. The responsibility for the provision of this service was placed with both the local health and welfare authorities, and it is within this context, Martin Bulmer (1987) contends, that 'Community Care' first appeared in official terminology, within the Royal Commission's 1957 report on Mental Illness and Mental Deficiency.

However, from the 1960s onwards the post-war consensus began to break up and there was a shift in emphasis within community care policies towards community involvement. In 1978 the DHSS defined community care in the mental health field as 'multi-faceted and multi-disciplinary, involving not only those responsible for providing statutory health and social services but also the family, voluntary bodies and, in fact, the whole community itself (DHSS 1978: 10). This new direction in community care policy, therefore, involved a move away from care 'in the community' to care 'by the community' (Bulmer 1987). This transformation was further developed with the advent of the 1979 Conservative government which had an ideological commitment to a reduction in public expenditure and the creation of a residual role for state welfare.

The government embarked upon a series of reviews of welfare as part of its drive to reduce public expenditure. This transition from care in the community to care by the community was clearly identified in the government's 1981 White Paper *Growing Older* which was concerned with community resources:

> The primary sources of support and care for elderly people are informal and voluntary. These spring from the personal ties of kinship, friendship and neighbourhood. They are irreplaceable. It is the role of public authorities to sustain, and where necessary, develop - but never to displace - such support and care. Care in the community must increasingly mean care by the community. (1981c: 3)

As early as 1981, therefore, the shift in the relationship between the state and 'private' carers within the community was clearly recognisable. The implementation of community care policies accelerated during the 1980s. This was due to the continuing programme of large hospital closures; the continued economic crisis; a concern to cap the rise in private residential care which was escalating and being met through social security payments, and the government's ideological commitment to such policy. Arguments were now being presented that care by the community was the best and most cost-effective form of care, and the government exhorted the moral values of individual responsibility and social obligation to underpin its ideological commitment. In addition, Webb and Wistow argue, the government relied on three comforting myths:

> that people have become neglectful of their social obligations to kin and neighbours and that a vast reservoir of informal care can be tapped simply by enforcing these obligations; that 'genuinely voluntary' provision, staffed by volunteers and paid for by charitable giving, can be rekindled with little difficulty; and that people can afford to buy services privately (Webb and Wistow, 1987: 93).

The notion that community care was 'a good thing' was increasingly being challenged by feminists who argued that: 'in practice community care equals care by the family, and in practice care by the family equals care by women' (Pascall 1986: 87). But for the government community care, and more specifically, the informal private care provided primarily by daughters and daughters-in-law, became an alternative solution to economic and demographic ills:

> The burden of taxation and the proportion of GNP distributed through the state were regarded as barriers to economic health as well as being undesirable in themselves. If these burdens were to be shifted - particularly in the context of rising numbers of elderly people - an alternative source of help would need to be identified: informal care was the obvious one (Twigg 1994: 5).

By the middle of the 1980s there was a further shift in the discourse on community care. John Baldock and Clare Ungerson described it in the following terms:

> This new discourse is self-consciously tough-minded, practical economistic and untroubled by linguistic niceties. It is represented in the blunt and anonymous writing of the documents that are making the running in the social policy debate these days...The new discourse we term 'managerialist' (Baldock and Ungerson 1991: 138).

This new emphasis in government direction had been influenced by the growth of the doctrine of New Public Management which had arisen in the 1980s. This doctrine aimed at slowing down or reversing public spending trends and 'shifting responsibility away from 'core' government institutions' (Hood 1991). The reports and reviews which were produced from the middle of the 1980s, therefore, constructed principles for the adoption of a 'market' style philosophy within community care. As will be seen in Chapter 8, there was an increasing focus upon economy, efficiency, effectiveness and value for money.

The main reports and reviews to be influenced by this shift in emphasis were: the 1986 Audit Commission's report entitled *Making a Reality of Community Care*, which looked at the progress of the implementation of community care and assessed whether it was offering value for public money; the 1988 Griffiths Report entitled *Community Care: Agenda for Action*, which reviewed the way in which public funds could be used to support community care policy; and the government's 1989 White Paper *Caring for People: Community Care in the Next Decade and Beyond*, which responded to the Griffiths Report and produced the policy for the future of community care.

The findings of the 1986 Audit Commission's report gave out some serious warnings to the government and concluded that present community care policies were neither cost effective or offering value for money.

The 1988 Griffiths Report

Sir Roy Griffiths approached his review through the doctrine of New Public Management and Consumerism. He took the findings of the 1986 Audit Commission's report as essential facts upon which to build. This included the Audit Commission's conclusion that: 'Although the money being spent should be adequate to provide at least as much improved level of community based services, the methods for distributing it do not match the requirements of community care policies' (Audit Commission 1986). The reforms, therefore, were to be achieved within the existing level of resources. Most importantly, he also took as his 'starting point' the notion of the residual role for the state and the primary function of the informal sector, which includes private carers:

> Publicly provided services constitute only a small part of the total care provided to people in need. Families, friends and neighbours and other local people provide the majority of care in response to needs which they are uniquely well placed to identify and respond to. This will continue to be the primary means by which people are enabled to live normal lives in community settings. The proposals take as their starting point that this is as it should be (Griffiths Report 1988: para. 3.2)

One of his most significant recommendations was the transfer of responsibility for community care to local authorities. This would involve a transformation of their role from service providers to 'enablers' and 'purchasers' of services. Central to this proposal, as will be particularly seen in Chapter 8, was the development of a 'contract culture' where local authorities would enter into contracts with service providers and stimulate a 'mixed economy of care', incorporating a diverse range of service providers to meet people's individual needs. A central implicit component of such provision was to come from the services of private carers.

The incorporation of private carers into this new world of contracts has been presented by Griffiths as 'unproblematic'. The assumptions contained within their positioning within the 'mixed economy of care' ensures that the task of caring for elderly, frail relatives will fall particularly heavily upon daughters and daughters-in-law within the gendered hierarchy of private caring relationships identified in the previous section.

Private carer's positioning within this transformation of community care policy is, however, paramount to the success of the reforms, and as such Griffiths acknowledges that 'the first task of publicly provided services is to support and where possible strengthen the network of carers' (Griffiths Report 1988: para. 3.2). The feminist critique of this declaration, however, suggests rather that:

> Carers were seen as a resource whose 'price' to social care agencies was very low: they only needed to put in small amounts of formal resources to ensure extensive inputs. Supporting carers represented a highly cost-effective strategy...The argument was rarely expressed in its most naked form, whereby the *only* reason to alleviate the circumstances of a carer was in order to ensure that he or she continued to give care (Twigg 1994: 6). [original italics].

The Griffiths report, therefore, builds upon and reinforces the social construction of a moral imperative to care through the ideological constructs of 'social obligation'. The ideological underpinning structuring this assumption is that it will be women, primarily white, middle class women and their daughters and daughters-in-law who will fulfil this function.

The reforms therefore place women increasingly within a dependent situation, especially if the caring of elderly relatives entails the eventual loss of paid employment for such daughters or daughters-in-law. It is not only a loss of income that such women will incur but also potential loss of pension rights and future career opportunities, and for some, although not all, a possible loss of personal identity and self-worth through their resulting social isolation.

Other social policy analysts and academic feminists have criticised the Griffiths report from the perspective of 'citizenship' and 'rights', pointing out the relative powerlessness of carers within these proposals, as opposed to other legislation:

> the report risks the occasional acknowledgement of carers but for the most part regards them as an unquestioned part of the 'given world within which community care will take place'. Considerably greater rights to assessment and support for carers is given in the Disabled Persons Act 1986 (Baldwin and Parker 1989).

The Griffiths proposals then also highlight a tension and contradiction within the notion of consumerism: the tension between carers sovereignty and choice and user sovereignty and choice.

The 1989 White Paper, 'Caring for People'. and the 1990 NHS and Community Care Act.

Many of the proposals contained within the Griffiths Report finally appeared in the publication of the government's White Paper and the 1990 Act, which, however, did not come fully into effect until April 1993. Local Authorities were charged with the responsibility for planning and co-ordinating the provision of community care. The key policy objective of the Act was that of enabling people to live independent lives, wherever possible in their own homes and the stated goals of choice and independence underlie the whole of the Act. Local Authorities were required to produce annual community care plans outlining their plans for implementing community care locally.

Private informal carers were accorded an elevated position within the White Paper not only through the acknowledgement that carers need help and support if they are to continue in their caring role; but through the inclusion of carers in the six key objectives for implementation of community care: 'to ensure that service providers make practical support for carers a high priority' (DoH 1989: para. 1.11). The Act itself also recognised carers formally within the official language of legislation and lays an obligation upon local authorities to consult with carers about service planning and provision.

The reforms and 'choice' for private carers

The reforms' emphasis upon managerialism and consumer choice has, as already noted, particular tensions for private carers. The findings of a critical study recently undertaken of the social construction of the private carer within the reforms, and within the language of a selection of local authorities' 1992/3 and 1993/4 Community Care Plans (Thompson 1993), confirms such tensions and contradictions. The study found that while the doctrine of new public management positively engages with, and supports, private carers through an instrumental and technocratic view of welfare; this was based upon a rational and essentialist notion of the 'normality' of private carers as 'service providers', rather than as 'consumers' in their own right.

This tension is particularly pertinent in view of the government's decree, due to limited resources, that services must be geared to those 'most in need'. The inference of this 'rationing' of services, as we have seen in Chapter 6, is that it will, in all probability, be the growing number of the elderly who will be 'the most in need': those parents requiring the 'heavy end' of caring; the long-term, physically demanding 'tending' tasks, which frequently take a toll upon the health of those carrying out the caring role, and which the government is assigning to the 'caring' daughters and daughters-in-law to take responsibility for, rather than the state. This throws into relief the question of carers' access to services in their own right, to meet their needs, which potentially may be in conflict with the cared-for person's needs.

The identification of this instrumental 'normative' discourse, in addition to the existing 'moral' imperative discourse based on 'social obligation', might, the study suggests, effectively collapse the question of choice for private carers to one position only, namely that of choosing 'to care'. For daughters or daughters-in-law to attempt to choose not to care, or to take the decision to stop caring, would be to go against the norms the reforms were attempting to impose; to go against patriarchal hegemony, and put the responsibility back on the state.

Summary

It has been argued that community care has undergone a transformation in relation to state intervention and regulation in Britain between the post-war period and the 1990s. The driving force of this transformation has been the New Right political ideology of consecutive conservative governments who have harnessed the political doctrine of new public management to help create a residual role for the state. The outcome of this policy has been an attempt to place the responsibility for care upon the 'informal sector', particularly 'the family'.

Such policy is built upon a particular ideological construct of patriarchal 'familial ideology' comprising a white 'male breadwinner' with a white 'dependent' wife and children. The assumption is that the family will be the 'first line of support for dependent kin'. The feminist critique of such policy argues that women are always 'defined in relation to men' (Carabine 1992: 28), and in effect, therefore, it will primarily be the wives, daughters and daughters-in-law who will take on this caring role while the husbands, sons and sons-in-law provide the economic resources to enable such support to happen. Furthermore, the construction of this familial ideology is based upon an androcentric, heterosexual and ethnocentric view of social relations which effectively masks the changing and diverse nature of families today, and reduces other family forms to the margins of mainstream social and welfare policy.

The question is, then, will this recent social construction of women, and particularly daughters and daughters-in-law, as private carers forming the first line of support for their elderly, ill, frail or disabled relatives command hegemonic power, or is it out of line with contemporary familial relations?

Empirical research into kinship obligations and responsibilities

Recent empirical research throws some light on to whether people see the family as the first line of support and whether there is a 'crisis in care' in families today. Finch and Mason's work looked at the questions of kin responsibility and obligations but in a wider context than the care of disabled, frail or elderly dependent relatives. Their basic premise is that 'kin responsibilities have negotiated as well as normative elements' (Finch and Mason 1993: 12). They argue that at a public level people in the late 1980s:

> were not acknowledging clearly identifiable principles about what kinds of assistance family members should offer each other. There is no evidence of a clear acknowledgement at this public normative level that families should be the first line of support for their members (*ibid*: 21).

At this public level, therefore, relatives were not acknowledging that they have clear responsibilities based on obligations. There was an indication, however, that responsibilities between parents and their children were 'accorded special status' and that, at the practical level of supporting kin, these responsibilities involved complex processes of negotiation rather than following fixed rules of obligation.

These processes of negotiation revolved around central themes, some of which are: reciprocity, particularly the importance of obtaining a balance of power between dependence-independence within the reciprocal relationship; 'developing commitments', a process which takes place over long period of time; an individual's personal 'biography' and 'reputation' within the kin group; and finally, making legitimate excuses (not to care). The question of responsibility then, Finch and Mason argue, rests not on rules of obligation, right or duty: 'our data shows a particularly strong resistance to the idea that anyone has a right to claim assistance from a relative. This is one of the strongest messages in our data '(*ibid*: 166). Rather, they state, kin responsibilities are fluid, unfixed and created primarily through the process of developing commitments over time. Sometimes these may only be half recognised and not consciously planned. They do, however, take on a moral dimension. It is possible, therefore, they state to see how the role of gender becomes entwined in the structural location of individuals; how 'women, who conventionally are seen as having time more readily available than men, are more likely to get locked into sets of commitments which entail giving time and labour'(*ibid*: 169). However, they warn this is not a simplistic process:

> We feel that we cannot say that in practice someone accepts a responsibility 'because' she is a woman - or even because she is a daughter - when there is so much variation and when people themselves do not present their actions in that way...Being a daughter is only part of what constitutes someone's effective structural position. One daughter may have accumulated a far more extensive range of commitments than others, even her own sisters, and these form part of the structural position which a woman occupies at any point in her life (*ibid*: 175).

This exploration of Finch and Mason's work helps to illuminate the complex and diverse processes underpinning the 'caring relationship' referred to earlier in this chapter. And although their findings potentially offer mothers, daughters and daughters-in-laws a degree of autonomous agency in deciding whether or not to care, it still recognises that the wider structural location of women within the domestic sphere may mean that 'they are more likely than men to begin on a path...where they start to develop sets of reciprocal responsibilities with kin' (*ibid*: 176). Their work also helps to show how the complex processes involved in the development of 'commitments over time' results in one particular daughter, rather than, say, an older or younger sister, 'taking up' the caring role.

Their study also offers possible explanations for why the current government may be concerned about a potential 'crisis in the family'. Their findings clearly indicated that people in Britain in the 1980s do not think the family should be seen as the first and primary source of support. In connection with caring for elderly dependants, the following example from their research illustrates this statement:

> In questions about caring for someone who cannot fully look after themselves, our respondents were more likely to accord responsibility to relatives if the assistance needed was temporary, or did not demand high levels of skill. But in questions which implied that the person needed nursing care, including intimate bodily contact, more people were inclined to say that the state services were preferable to relatives (*ibid*: 19).

Further insights into changing attitudes towards care for older people in Europe have been identified in a recent study undertaken by McGlone and Cronin. Some of their key findings indicate that although the traditional family has changed beyond all recognition within a number of European countries, there is no evidence as yet that families are less willing to care than they once were. The family is overwhelmingly seen as the main source of care for older people, and that women are by far the main supporters. However, there was evidence that families may be less willing to care for elderly relatives suffering from senile dementia (McGlone and Cronin 1994).

Their study also identified changing attitudes towards care and patterns of care preferences which were particularly relevant to the themes of this chapter. They found that daughters and daughters-in-law now 'weigh up' family obligations against decisions about employment, career and social security entitlements and that older people themselves are increasingly expressing a preference for professional care over family care, especially if it requires a long term commitment. Additionally, in a British Gallup poll survey three out of five people over 65 stated that the responsibility for their care should shift to the state (*ibid*).

Other studies, however, point to class and racial differences within kinship relationships. This is particularly pertinent to Black elders now experiencing the effects of poor employment prospects for kin, and tightening immigration controls, whereby they are left with no access to informal caring networks (Fenton 1985; Gunaratnam 1993). Hilary Graham, too takes up this point to demonstrate the advantages white middle class women have over other women in accessing care:

> Many white working-class women and Black and ethnic minority women have found their care arrangements structured by employment opportunities and immigration restrictions in ways that restrict their opportunity to receive and give care within their families (Graham 1993a: 131).

To conclude this section the following example from work in progress by this author on the question of how much choice private carers feel they have to say 'no' to caring, illustrates some of the dilemmas and theories raised in this chapter. A daughter, herself a grandmother, caring for her elderly mother who needs twenty-four hours attention a day is feeling at crisis point, and wants to stop the caring role:

> My mum don't owe me a thing, but at the same token I don't think I owe my mum... But I need help to cope with how I'm feeling, and whichever way you turn there doesn't seem to be much for the carer....I don't want to pile the blame on my brother. Why he doesn't come, he's got so many outside interests, that is the only thing I can think of. Perhaps he's doing what I should have done years ago, but I set a pattern and I can't seem to break it .

In summary, the findings from these examples of contemporary empirical research enable the debate about 'who cares' to move away from a biologically determinist injunction to one which encompasses a social constructionist framework. Such a framework potentially offers a degree of relative autonomy and agency for daughters and daughters-in-law within the gendered patriarchal structure of social relations. This is also tempered, however, by other factors such as age, class and race.

Conclusions

Evidence has been presented in this chapter that recent social policy has been consistently formulated on an out-moded androcentric and ethnocentric social construction of 'the family'. This model has not acknowledged the actual diversity and differences which exist within families today; nor has it taken account of an 'established feminist critique and a newly emerging "anti-racist" critique' (Williams 1989: 37). Part of this critique is the growing recognition of the differential experiences of women; the recognition that women experience oppression differently according to age, race, and class.

Coupled with this is the findings from recent empirical research that indicates there is a growing body of evidence pointing towards changing attitudes towards caring. This does not necessarily mean that families are not willing to care, or that 'caring is in crisis', but that the 'taking up' of the caring role is becoming increasingly contingent upon other factors. One such factor is the increasing number of women in the workforce, another is the possible beginning of a breakdown of 'perceived' traditional roles, as evidenced by Janet Finch and Jennifer Mason.

Such attitudes offer, at least potentially, the opportunity for daughters and daughters-in-law scope for 'choice' and acknowledge the intersection of the public and the private. It is possible then, that current community care policy, rather than supporting and reinforcing the forms of bonds to which parents and their children aspire, may be running the risk of undermining such bonds through constructing the private carer in a role to which neither biological ties nor cultural expectations conform. Increasingly, daughters may come to deny or resist mainstream social policy's current imperative to become 'daughters of the reforms'.

8 'Contracting out' familial liabilities

Richard Common

> In fact we were our own social services department, our own social workers, meals on wheels, community advisers, dial-a-bus service - indeed, we provided mutual support of a kind now clumsily and expensively run by local authorities.
>
> (Norman Tebbit (1989) commenting on life in Hemel Hempstead in the late 1950s.)

This chapter attempts to outline the major questions raised by the marketisation of social services, which is somewhat different from the voluntarism lauded by Tebbit. Community care (the policy, not the concept) appears to have its roots in New Right solutions to 'better' government. The chapter begins by discussing how community care was placed on the government agenda and then implemented. It then moves on to discuss the key consequences of how the policy has impacted on the choices of social service users and their families, with particular reference to the growth of residential care, the blurring of the health and social care boundary and the promotion of choice. Finally, the chapter will assess the implications that the contractorisation of social services has on familial liabilities. This assessment is linked to the insistence that the market will provide services based on the assumption that individuals, or family units, should take responsibility for the choices about the care they, or members of their families, receive.

Formulating community care

An ideological faith in the supremacy of market mechanisms in supplying social services more efficiently and effectively than the public sector has underpinned this major reform of social services. A decade ago, George and Wilding (1985) noted that 'anti-collectivism' was the dominant ideology in nineteenth century Britain. The renaissance of anti-collectivism can be traced to the break down of the 'post-war political consensus' which started to show signs of strain in the 1960s. Faith in the primacy of market mechanisms over government in the allocation of resources lead to growing hostility to the Welfare State amongst the nascent 'New Right' in the 1970s. George and Wilding (1985) summarise the critique of welfarism offered by the new right:

> They see welfare state policies as threatening or damaging to central social values and institutions - the family, work incentives, economic development, individual freedom, for example - and in general they are opposed to provision which is more than minimal. (*ibid*: 35)

A more particular criticism of the welfare state is the belief that government is inherently inefficient because it lacks competition. Government agencies are monopoly suppliers of services. The New Right view sees families as being more or less lulled into choosing expensive or inappropriate care simply because the state provides it. The state, in effect, was seen as depriving families of choice over social care and the New Right was pledged to restoring the primacy of the family as a 'decision making' unit, rather than the bureaucracy. Community care looks set to alter the pattern of parent-offspring relations by increasing the involvement of families in choices about care, whether it be choosing a residential home for elderly relatives or young children with physical or learning difficulties.

Within the context of the New Right agenda, when viewed against the successive post-1979 Conservative reforms of the public sector, social services policy seems neither radical nor particularly neo-liberal. Cochrane (1993) thinks that it is too simplistic to dismiss community care as part of a coherent New Right agenda. Indeed, according to Henwood *et al* (1991) 'community care has been a national policy objective for at least the last thirty years' and Dunleavy traces community care back to 1961, when the process of running down large mental hospitals began (citing Brindle, 1988). Also, the way in which care is delivered has changed: 'in addition, children's homes have given way to fostering, and old people's homes to greater provision of services for the elderly in their own homes'. However, the process has been generally slow because insufficient funding has been supplied to provide full alternative facilities (Wistow 1985, cited in Dunleavy).

'Community care' is a vague and often contentious term. Community care is not simply about allowing people to be cared for in their own homes rather than in drab long-stay institutions. The fragmentation of social service provision, which is at the heart of the 1990 NHS and Community Care Act, plus the shift away from long-stay institutional care, has provided Conservative administrations with an excellent opportunity to subject local government units to the discipline of the market. Individuals are supposedly better placed to make choices about the care they receive in their own homes rather than in long-stay residential care.

Furthermore, the New Right see the welfare state as fundamentally damaging to the long-term interests of people (see George and Wilding *op cit*). 'Community care' has always been provided by the family and neighbours, the type of ideal which Tebbit refers to above. The New Right would argue that should this informal network break down, or a person or family are in a position to choose through purchasing power, the voluntary sector or the market will provide the necessary care. Community care places social services departments (SSDs) as part of this network; as a 'broker' acting between clients and the non-statutory sector.

Instrumental in achieving this 'mixed economy' for care was to encourage domiciliary care, wherever possible, as the preferred alternative to long-stay institutionalisation. The term 'community care' usually refers to this process. However, community care is perceived as a manifestation of the general shift in western liberal democratic welfare states towards the scaling down of large-scale institutions run by governments. If the former clients of these institutions are unable to be maintained in their own homes, then residential care should be provided by micro-agencies run by the non-government sector. The 'mixed economy' of welfare is thus promoted by this process (Wistow *et al* 1994) where the public sector competes with the non-government sector (which includes a myriad of organisational forms) to provide services for clients.

The concept of a 'community care' policy was a rare instance of consensus politics in the Thatcher era. Wistow *et al* (1994) remark how support for the White Paper was 'universal'. This consensus was largely based on the recognition that clients of large-scale institutions 'are entitled to live in the least restrictive environment necessary and (to) live their lives as normally and independently as they can' (Lerman 1982, quoting the US General Accounting Office). If clients are 'entitled', who has the duty to provide a normal or independent life for them? Community care implies that funding for social care should not be used to guarantee the continuity of large-scale public provision but instead should go to community-based agencies in either the voluntary or private sectors (Dunleavy 1991).

It could even be argued that talk about opening social services to the market was merely an ideological gloss to what many believed was a pragmatic reform of social services. However a rationale for community care is 'dressed up', the fact remains that the costs of providing care is rapidly escalating, especially services to elderly people, and the phenomenon is global. One impetus towards community care, when placed within the context of public expenditure constraint, came partly from the pressure on social security spending for residential care for the elderly. Clearly, it was not simply enough to rely on the private sector to 'take the strain' in the direct provision of residential care.

Evidence from the United States suggests that the notion that government is increasingly shouldering the community care burden is a myth. Tennstedt and McKinlay (1989) pointed to a number of studies which found a remarkable 75 per cent of 'impaired' elderly people relied entirely on family and friends as their *sole* source of support, with only 26% of formal care for this group funded by the government. Tennstedt and McKinlay concluded that 'clearly, the vast majority of long-term care is provided informally, and privately, at no public cost'. In the UK, a DHSS report on community care in 1981 had noted that successful community care packages depended upon the shouldering of financial burdens by informal carers.

If community care can be viewed as a process of 'deinstitutionalization', fiscal restraint will be realised by diverting budgetary increments away from SSDs to 'private organizations, or to community-based provision' (Dunleavy 1991). The Ridley doctrine (Ridley 1988) of the enabling local authority saw local authorities as multi-purpose organisations able to write contracts with the non-government sector to provide a range of services. Local authorities would continue to finance social services but no longer provide them. Contracting out social care is part of the shift to the 'mixed economy' or what Dunleavy (1991) describes as the 'multi-sourced production of public services'. The apparent superiority of private sector management coupled with New Right argument about rivalry being the key to cost effectiveness gave the policy appeal at the centre of government and convinced Conservative controlled local authorities at least, that contracting would be cheaper than providing services directly.

Introducing community care

Despite the currency of New Right ideas in the 1980s it appears that the momentum towards a substantive community care 'policy' only really began in 1986. The publication of the Audit Commission report *Making a Reality of Community Care* (1986) pointed to a number of areas where fundamental problems lay. The report found that savings from community care were "fairly modest, since much domiciliary and smaller-scale care is relatively expensive". The government reacted by appointing Sir Roy Griffiths to examine community care expenditure and to make recommendations where spending would be more efficient and effective.

Sir Roy Griffiths' track record in the public sector was already impressive. Earlier in the 1980s he had introduced the concept of *general management* into the NHS. Griffiths report *Agenda for Action* was published in 1988 and laid the foundations for the managerial, cultural and organisational changes that were finally implemented in April 1993 after being refined by the government's own proposals in the White Paper *Caring for People* (1989). The first practical guides or 'policy guidance' for local authorities appeared later the same year and in 1991 *Purchase of Service* (1991) stated that:

> The Government believes that there are a number of ways SSDs can promote the mixed economy of care. These include inviting tenders from private and voluntary organisations; stimulating the establishment of "not for profit" agencies; facilitating the creation of self managing units; and encouraging new voluntary sector activity.

Not only are SSDs required to contract out services wherever possible, they also need to take the lead in actively stimulating the non-statutory sector. The contractorisation of community care has meant that social services departments assess potential clients and then *purchase* the necessary services to meet their needs. Potentially, services can be bought from anyone who is prepared to sell, subject to adequate quality controls and assurance. SSDs may continue to *provide* services directly or from the non-statutory sector if there is adequate supply. With the government stipulation that 85 per cent of community care funding be spent in the non-statutory sector, such a broad-brush requirement will fail to take into account local market conditions (for instance, see Common and Flynn 1992).

What does the 'mixed economy' look like? Who is in the non-statutory sector? Hoggett and Taylor (1993) came up with a useful typology of organisations based on ownership: private; family-, owner-, or labour- managed; donor-owned (charitable trusts or more informal groups); beneficiary-owned (self-help, self-advocacy); community-owned; and hybrid organisations (joint statutory/non-statutory ventures). However, if any of these types of organisations enters into a block contract with the local authority, do they all become 'hybrid' organisations at the blurring of the public-private interface if the majority of their funding comes from the government? SSDs remain key players in the mixed economy.

Most local authorities have now divided their SSDs into separate purchasing and providing organisations in accordance with the Act, but this presents immediate challenges for moves towards a *user-orientated* service. SSD staff who assess a client are not likely to care for them. Effectively, the role of the SSD has shifted to a large extent from that of provider to that of 'enabler', in accordance with the Ridley doctrine, while retaining the local authority's importance as an elected body whose staff serve the needs of the public. Also part of the SSD's new enabling role is to make their staff 'mediators' of care, as purchasers of care they will have to balance conflicting opinions within families with the range of provision available. A key problem is how to make services *user-orientated* through services delivered by a contract entered into on the user's behalf.

Also, the import of generic management language and debate, which forms the backcloth to much of the post-1979 public sector reforms, may be usefully applied here. For instance, Normann (1991) refers to the 'increasing integration between the functions of production and consumption' when drawing upon Toffler's *Third Wave* predictions. Very briefly, Toffler felt that society and industry were undergoing such fundamental changes that individuals would inevitably become 'prosumers', an idea that Normann uses to underpin his arguments around the importance of client as coproducer. User and carer involvement in the production of contracts is explicit in government guidance (Department of Health Social Services Inspectorate 1991). This may take several forms such as user representation on the advisory or management committees of provider organisations or consultation at the service specification development stage. Is community care at the edge of the 'prosumerist' movement? In reality, much user involvement in the production of services is conducted on an *ad hoc* basis, with little consensus as to how users and carers can get involved with service planning and delivery (Wistow *et al* 1994; Flynn and Hurley 1993)

Despite the apparent retention of local authorities as direct service providers where the market cannot provide (or 'enablers', arranging for service provision where the market is developed), the government presented funding problems following the formal implementation of community care in April 1993. For instance, late in 1994, stories in the Press appeared documenting how local authorities such as Gloucestershire and Lancashire were in crisis over community care funding. The transfer of the cost of residential and nursing care to local authorities effectively meant there was a finite allocation of resources which replaced the open-ended budget to social security. Recently, the Association of County Councils have accused the Treasury of using the policy to make savings of £200 million (Prestage 1995). Within the context of strained local-central fiscal relations, where resource allocation has been increasingly centralised, local authorities (including SSDs) have lost sensitivity to local needs, a fundamental rationale for community care.

Issues

There are some key issues concerned with the requirement that SSDs contract out as many services as possible that have implications for the choice of care that families can make. The first of these is the apparently perverse expansion of residential care, which flies in the face of the fundamental tenets of *community care* but is an important side-effect of promoting the mixed economy. The implications for familial responsibilities are important ones, and have attracted media attention, to 'granny dumping' scandals for instance (see Chapter 6 above). Secondly, community care impinges on organisational boundaries, which is a source of concern for professionals, users and their families and carers. Thirdly, there are problems associated with the precepts of *community care* that promise to improve choice and accountability for service users.

The expansion of residential care

As part of the consensus on community care, it is generally accepted that residential or nursing home care is considered as a last resort when people can no longer be maintained in their own homes, even with the support of formal or informal care, without a serious deterioration in the quality of their lives. Although *Caring for People* (Department of Health, 1989) included residential care as part of a 'spectrum' of community care, the White Paper was keen to stress the development of non-residential forms of care. Governmental preference for placing people in non-residential care appears to be resource driven given that many people choose this form of care for a number of reasons. However, there has been a paradoxical expansion in the residential sector. For certain clients and their families, long-stay hospital accommodation may be preferable to uncertain residential care regimes (including doubts about staff qualifications etc.) or to relieve informal caring duties of relatives.

Adult placement schemes, although falling into the category of 'residential care' may be one solution which balances the needs of users and their families and the resources of the Department of Health. Such schemes, where users are referred to as 'guests' are cheaper than residential accommodation and lack the stringency found in formal residential homes. The formal residential sector continues to suffer wide variations in good practice and Walker (1991) points to a number of research studies that have found many instances of where users are denied the 'freedom, privacy and comfort' they would expect in their own homes and management is 'often strict and rigid'. However, 'guest' schemes are still regarded as innovatory and so are less easy to specify in contracts so the preference remains for the private and nursing home residential sectors. Formal residential care is less of a problem for contract writers and monitors as residential care regimes can be subjected to rules and uniformity that are easier to codify in a service specification. Greater management resources are more likely to be invested in the contracting process if the care regime becomes more tailored to individual needs, but at a greater financial cost to the local authority.

The residential care 'boom' happened between 1980 and 1990 when private beds increased from 37,400 to 155,600 and nursing home beds increased from 26,900 to 123,100 (Henwood 1992). Economic recession in the early 1990s undoubtedly dampened this expansion yet the balance between quality care in the community and encouraging the private sector (rather than the voluntary/non-profit sector) remains towards the latter. A further impetus to the expansion of the private sector came in 1988 with the introduction of income support. For example, Hereford and Worcester County Council was motivated into contracting with the Birmingham Council for Old People in order to save money because residents would have access to social security funding whereas residents in local authority homes are denied this financial support (Davies and Edwards 1990). Furthermore, *Caring for People* provided a direct incentive for local authorities to seek economies in their own provision of residential care resulting in the 'hotel' costs of residents in the non-statutory sector being supported by the social security system, but in local authority accommodation those same costs would have to be paid for by the local authority itself.

So much for residential care as a 'last resort'. If 'institutionalization' is encouraged through the suppression of public costs, then it can only encourage family members to offload awkward personal care tasks (which gives rise to the 'granny dumping' phenomenon). George and Maddox (1989), having reviewed US research, argue that the timing of residential care placement is determined by 'family caretakers'. This happens when residential care is considered as an option when family members are no longer able to provide care, or tolerate providing care. Hard pressed GPs may play a role in acquiescing to family demands. Of course, ultimately residential care may be in the best interests of all concerned, but those with close relatives, especially daughters, are less likely than others to enter residential care (Walker 1991). Feminists are unhappy with these assumptions, and question the social constructs that assert adult daughters feel a strong duty to care for elderly parents. This is not helped when Conservative governments imply that this is 'correct' behaviour (Foster 1991) and fits with the 'family values' of the radical right.

However, in the area of residential child care there has been a real decline stimulated by the growth of foster care, although adolescents are more likely to be in residential care than children. In adolescent care, the trend is towards small-scale provision. (Cotton and Hellinckx 1994). Changes in child care practice have seen an increasing involvement of the family in the care process with more emphasis placed on parents exercising their rights and participating in decisions about their children. Hence, alternatives to residential care for children have been stimulated by contractorisation under community care policy such as day centres, centres for independent living under supervision and centres for home-based treatment.

Social care or health care?

Promoting the mixed economy can blur accountability. According to an *Independent on Sunday* article (Jones 1993) 'the scope for professional buck-passing is almost infinite, given the variety of professionals who are supposed to take a role in their care and, more seriously, the inadequate resources at their disposal'. The problem is that community care demands an inter-agency approach. The 1990 NHS and Community Care Act drew upon the two 1989 White Papers *Working For Patients* (relating to the NHS) and *Caring for People* (relating to the Social Services). The stress on inter-agency working implicit in the Act is a key impetus to the marketisation of community care, but this approach is beset by problems. Nocon (1994) points to the 'grey' area between social and health care as one such problem, and quoting Berman *et al* (1990), he is concerned that the contractorisation of social services is leading to 'specified and inflexible services, with users potentially falling into the gaps between organisations or their contracts'.

Caring for People did attempt to specify the responsibilities of both local and health authorities but Sally Hornby's *Collaborative Care* (1993) points to a key problem in community care implementation which is the co-ordination of care over organisational boundaries. Joint purchasing arrangements are not a simple solution to this problem, indeed it may even exacerbate collaborative efforts if co-ordination is poor. This is a challenge faced by the enabling authorities especially when writing contracts with the kind of flexibility that allows clients some degree of self-determination over who looks after them. The White Paper had called for collaboration between service providers when contract specifications are drawn up. However, Hornby makes the point that the contract between client and carer is usually verbal; which can cause management nightmares for case managers. Where the 'user' is a family, Hornby says that children should be encouraged to become part of the contract-making process.

Joint working is mandatory for community care planning, acute hospital discharges, admissions to nursing homes and the use of the Mental Health Specific Grant. But for contracts to operate smoothly and sensitively, communication between the two statutory authorities (i.e., the local authority and the district health authority) need conducting properly. As both local and health authorities are essentially multi-purpose organisations, joint communication may not have a high priority. For instance, local authorities had to consider the Children Act as well as setting up 'arms length' inspection units and complaints procedures alongside community care implementation. On the other hand, proponents of health service reforms would argue that health authorities are no longer subject to political short-termism given that district health authorities now lack local political control, unlike SSDs.

This 'shifting distinction' between health care and social care can leave elderly people, in particular, and their families with unexpected financial burdens, especially where elderly people have been discharged from hospital. Money for residential care that has been transferred to the local authority has come from the social security budget: individuals can 'top up' any shortfall between assessment for means-tested benefits and the actual cost of residential care. Clients who receive income support are often unable to do this and rely on the discretion of adult children or other relatives in meeting the difference.

The amount of money local authorities receive is based on an estimate of the equivalent social security payments to support clients in residential or nursing home care. In the first year of community care implementation (1993/4), local authorities were 'to receive £399m in transferred funds to purchase community care services' (Flynn and Hurley 1993). Further pressure on families to 'top up' has come from many non-statutory providers deliberately raising their charges above income support levels. Many elderly people devote all their benefits to fee payments leading to dismal scenarios such as the one described by Sinclair and Brown (1991) where 'proprietors now hand on clothes from deceased residents to current ones in straitened circumstances'. It should be pointed out that only married partners of people needing care are liable to contribute directly topping up residential fees, but other family members do contribute. In these circumstances, care management is really about assessing the ability to pay.

Choice and accountability

Community care is supposed to enhance choice and clarify lines of accountability for the service user, despite the problems of co-ordination described above. However, we return to the problem of resources. Regarding clients as 'customers' assumes economic purchasing power on behalf of the client. However, client's families may have purchasing power even if the client does not. If this is the case, who chooses? Furthermore, it makes a nonsense of the drive towards a user-centred service if SSDs are driven into negotiating the cheapest possible (within quality constraints) deals with providers. Flynn and Hurley point to the dangers of wedding parsimony to a needs-driven service:

> In the new system local authorities have to arrange a system of care management to assess people's needs and target the cash-limited budgets

> towards those in greatest need. This rationing process implies that the assessment of need is tempered by the availability of cash. (1993: 5)

Implicit in the White Paper is that publicly provided residential care inevitably restricts user choice, and that care in the community is the best way of using restricted public funding, despite the fact that formal community care is not cheap intrinsically. As Allen *et al* (1992) point out that community care in many cases is only made possible by the existence of "extensive *informal* [my emphasis] care networks". The existence of informal care however is very often a consequence of a lack of choice in formal care settings, either because of budgetary strictures or the lack of a well developed market. Families don't necessarily choose to provide informal networks of care when they are denied access to the formal community care system.

The rationing process referred to by Flynn and Hurley (*op cit*) is indicative of the wider quasi-market reforms going on elsewhere in the public sector. Inevitably, the user faces marginal choices because bureaucrats or professionals act as 'brokers' for care, and those who are allowed access to care have it rationed. In community care these brokers are usually GPs and social workers, but they may include others such as community psychiatric nurses. The forum where choice is to be exercised is when the packages of care are assembled by the professionals, and here the user and his or her family are supposed to be able to negotiate this package jointly with the package assembler. A joint King's Fund Centre/Nuffield Institute report (1994) targeted G.Ps as the weakest link in the community care chain as they tended to be poorly involved and informed and some were found to be 'deliberately undermining new approaches by using hospital referrals to bypass liaising with social services'.

For professionals to act as brokers is essential for a parsimonious use of resources, or put rather more succinctly by Allen *et al* (1992): 'the question of money is very important in determining the extent to which people can exercise choice'. Two immediate limitations to choosing become clear, firstly, the income of the users (who are often entitled to state benefits that they are unaware of) and secondly, the budgets of the statutory services. Choice in the market place assumes purchasing power, and users of social services who do not have this power have to rely upon the professionals (who have the buying power) to make choices on their behalf. User purchasing power will only increase if their family chooses to contribute paying for some element of their care. Secondly, there is no rationality in the assembly of care packages. If community care is to provide the optimal level of care for the user, then the assembly process would begin with the *user's* choices.

Allen *et al* (1992) point to the difficulty of assessing whether or not packages of care are 'tailor-made' for the clients or whether services were merely added or deleted according to if they were available. They conclude that 'it was also difficult to assess whether the package was the *best* [my emphasis] design available', and that package assemblers took an incremental approach to package design. This does nothing for user choice on the one hand, or rational resource use on the other. Rather than empowering service users, users were more likely to feel at the mercy of an ad hoc system of resource allocation.

Although a lack of resources is clearly to blame here, it is only part of the explanation for the lack of rational care-package assembly. In a market, choice is only made possible by the flow of information from producers. In the quasi-market of community care, users are often reliant on their brokers for their information. If the care managers or other professionals lack market information, then the user cannot be exercising choice. As in real markets, brokers cannot have perfect information but in community care they are hampered by two factors. The first is the lack of a 'well developed data base of potential private and voluntary service providers into which they could tap' (Allen *et al*, 1992). Community care plans were supposed to supply this information to both brokers and users. Secondly, markets will vary in structure across the country, supply for one particular service may be plentiful in one urban area but may be completely absent in a rural county. Where there are local monopolies or oligopolies, suppliers may even want to limit the flow of information. Fixed-term contracts with single, powerful providers does little for user choice. Flynn and Hurley (1993) suggest that this can only be remedied by SSDs taking a more strategic approach before contract letting that includes techniques such as user surveys. Ideally, users should be involved at all stages of the contracting process.

Turning to the issue of accountability, a core public sector value is that the service user can hold politicians to account for poor service delivery. However, users may feel vulnerable when the services they receive are delivered partially or exclusively by the non-statutory sector. It is possible that because of this uncertainty, users may choose (where they can exercise choice) to receive directly provided local authority services rather than those provided by the private sector. However, other clients may come forward for community care to receive services from the non-statutory sector to avoid the 'social services stigma' (Common and Flynn 1992).

In the less certain quasi-market of community care, one solution to weak accountability chains is user involvement or moves towards user-centred services. Earlier, it was noted that voluntary organisations are particularly adept at ensuring users were represented either on advisory or management committees. Users may also be involved at the contract negotiation or service design stages. The private sector may be more reluctant at having users being party to commercial 'secrets' or making demands that might damage profitability, whereas firms in a competitive markets take the opposite view, where incorporation of customer's views may give them the competitive edge over rival suppliers.

Clearly, as noted earlier, choice of residential care depends on the ability of elderly people to pay the full cost of the place, or finding a third party (usually a family member) willing to pay the difference between a local authority's proposed placement and the chosen one. If families are unwilling to contribute, then people will be denied choice and compelled to stay at home or with their families. Families may prefer this to paying the difference. A mention should be made here of the Independent Living Fund (ILF). This is an initiative to put purchasing power in the hands of clients and offering them real choices about who provides care for them in their own home. After 1993, the ILF was devised to help support certain severely disabled people with relatively expensive care needs. Local authorities pay the first £200 per week but the scheme is dogged by bureaucratic problems (Strong 1994). Treasury fears are unlikely to result in an expansion of the ILF, which appears to be the closest to a user-led reform of social services.

Towards the contractorisation of familial liabilities

A key difficulty of contracting for community care is defining the 'user'. Because the public sector has multiple stake-holders (unlike the private sector), the 'user' is not simply the recipient of social services; the family, along with the community, politicians, council and income tax payers, all have a stake in the outcome of statutory services. This issue only becomes problematic once market-like conditions are brought to bear on social services as a consequence of community care implementation. The 'user' starts to become a 'customer' once the individual or their families begin to buy services that supplement formal care arrangements: it is care at a price. The problem is that caring relationships are not easy to fit into market assumptions, for instance, there is nothing particularly 'rational' about informal care. Earlier, Hornby pointed out that it is often the 'family' (rather than the individual service user) that becomes the service recipient and this can pose a problems for community care practitioners, especially in the field of child care or where carers have to make decisions on behalf of clients with severe disabilities. Conflicts of interest may begin to arise between family members.

There is potential for (implicit or explicit) multiple contractual relationships working side by side. A service contract will exist between the local or health authority purchaser and the service supplier, where user involvement should be sustained, or introduced where it is absent. A further contract should exist between the supplier and the user and his or her family, if this is appropriate. Many residential care homes already offer these kinds of local 'deals'. The fundamental question is whether democratic concepts of citizenship are undermined as contractorisation notionally abandons the unwritten contract between voter-as-service-user and politicians who arrange for service provision. However, users and their families, ultimately remain dependent upon care managers who retain the link with political accountability, if they lack their own purchasing power.

Unwritten contracts also exist between clients and their informal carers. These contracts are deeply ingrained in the social construction of the relationships amongst kinship groups. Studies have pointed to the existence of preference hierarchies (Tennstedt and McKinlay 1989 and Qureshi and Walker 1989) with the spouse at the top, followed by adult offspring down to friends and neighbours, with the stress on female carers. This socially constructed hierarchy may break down if formal services are more readily available, although Qureshi and Walker (1989) found no evidence to support this. The key issue then becomes a reassessment of the relationship between formal and informal care: as Tennstedt and McKinlay (1989) assert: 'it is not the case that informal care complements, or is ancillary to, formal services. Rather, formal services complement, or are ancillary to, a well-established, pervasive, and continuing informal system of care'. Community care policy appears designed to encourage families to initiate or continue care in order to deter family members from using statutory services. This misses the point that families provide care voluntarily. Furthermore, long-term socio-economic changes have meant that more women are working, and less happy to be designated as carers. Community care policy appears to rest on an increasingly flawed assumption that women will continue to be the primary source of informal care. Wicks (1991) adds to this list the move to smaller and mobile families and trends in divorce and remarriage as other impetuses that shake this assumption.

Another dilemma for the contractorisation of familial liabilities is the presumption that formal care can provide the same service as the family. If Qureshi and Walker's (1989) claim 'that informal care is prima facie preferable to recipients' should be taken seriously, then the issue of whether or not to contractorise familial liabilities centres on quality. Substituting informal care with formal care may result in a loss of quality for the client but the family would gain from losing awkward or inconvenient personal care roles. Families may still be able to offer emotional support which is often lacking in the roles of 'detached' professionals, but not all users could rely on this blend. Clearly, the financial incentives to the private sector, and increasingly, to the non-profit sector, do not sit comfortably with the incentive to provide services of a similar quality to that offered by the families themselves.

On the other hand, the formal sector offers advantages when it can offer greater resources and expertise than that supplied by the market or informally. Also, Qureshi and Walker (1989) note that the statutory sector can act in an impartial way, which can assuage family disputes. Core public sector values ensure that statutory services have an obligation to provide equal services for similar cases, which can still be discharged in the event of the incapacity of individual carers. This is a scenario which is difficult to contemplate in the informal sector where individuals are usually dependent upon one principal carer. Qureshi and Walker (1989) remark how informal care is part of the social construct whereas formal care is 'organised to be delivered to all people in particular defined categories of need: the disabled, children at risk, and so on'. This leads to another problem as the disciplines of contractorisation, including adherence to service specifications, has formalised much of the work process in the non-statutory sector (Common and Flynn 1992). Contracts tend to codify and reinforce care 'categories', which results in an inflexibility that does not fit easily with notions of freedom of choice. There is a further difficulty in mapping the boundary between formal and informal care and the grey area between the two is much the same as the one that exists between 'health' and 'social' care (outlined above). The contract culture has done much to blur the distinction as local authorities write contracts with micro-agencies, localised groups and the voluntary sector, whose outputs are hard to specify and where inappropriate referrals are more likely.

Scrivens (1992) argues that social policy fundamentally conflicts with the rationality of the market. The evidence suggests that the contracting out of familial liabilities is a theoretical impossibility on this criteria. There is nothing rational about the social constructs which surrounds the choices that users and their families make about the consumption of care, whether it is provided formally or informally. The care 'brokers' (the care managers and GPs) could be removed by giving clients and their families purchasing power, but any improvement in choice for users and decision making for families would only be marginal due to fundamental market imperfections. The contractorisation of familial liabilities will continue to be possible only for those families with the ability to pay, and not necessarily in the best interests of the family member who is being 'contracted out'.

Conclusions

The broad political consensus that began around community care in the 1980s becomes to look a little shaky from the perspective of the mid-1990s. In particular, concerns about the ageing of the elderly population coupled to wider market-led reforms in the public sector appear to have overridden the more pragmatic, 'community driven' rationales for the policy. Community care has been seized upon by the new right as an arena for testing deeply held convictions about the ability of market mechanisms to provide social care. On the other hand, community care has presented an opportunity for services to be user orientated, and contractorisation, if handled properly, can serve as an adjunct to this process. Furthermore, if a rationale for community care is the control of public money, support by the statutory sector for families who provide informal care will help save money by postponing indefinitely the likelihood of admission to residential care. Also, by offering respite to carers, who might otherwise suffer health problems, community care could save money in the long term.

However, a chief flaw in community care policy is that it assumes that carers are usually women. This assumption is widened into the belief that caring for its members is the responsibility of the family. In turn this has lead to the perception that 'social services substitute for rather than support families' (Walker 1991). Because the majority of carers are women, care managers will tend to allocate social services in preference to those users without wives or daughters. Clearly, carers have a stake in exercising choice as much as the people they care for, but - as has already been discussed in Chapter 7 - female carers are more likely to be denied this.

It is doubtful if the Tebbit utopia will ever exist. The social construction of the parent-offspring relationship is being increasingly fashioned within the constraints of economic hardship. Governments are less able to relieve the strain, irrespective of dominant ideologies, and the British government has embarked on a reform that nominally places families at the centre of decision making about social care their family members' need. In order that families benefit from community care, they should be able to negotiate within the market on an equal basis - from an empowered position. However, what is empowerment? If it is about having the money, it is the care managers who have the power. If it is about involvement in the decision making process, there are various gradations of how much power users and families can have in the decision making process. Only where there is choice, is there 'power' in the community care market. The imperfections of the market for care mean choice often remains limited and users remain dependent on the care managers who make care packages on their behalf, even if the system was to be generously funded. Should state intervention be limited to providing the resources and the forum where users and their caring family members write their own contracts for community care?

9 Conclusion: The limits of policy intervention

Hartley Dean

This book has been concerned to explore the nature, the extent and the effects of policy intervention in parent-offspring relations. At the time of writing, the declared priority of Britain's Conservative government is to 'transfer power and responsibility wherever appropriate from the state to the family' (Bottomley 1994). As we have seen, however, the realities of government policy belie this simplistic tenet. Such realities are rendered complex for at least three reasons. First, it is not clear that '*the* family' as a universal or unambiguous entity exists. Secondly, far from transferring power to families, government is often retaining the power to define and to impose very particular notions of responsibility. Thirdly, the purposes for which responsibilities are transferred to families are often ambiguous or contradictory.

In unpicking the themes contained within the chapters making up this volume, I shall be concerned, therefore, less with the contested concept of 'the family', than more specifically with relationships between parents and children. I shall also be concerned to examine critically the particular duties and debts with which policy makers are preoccupied. The principal themes upon which the chapter will concentrate are those of biology, history and ideology; the three dimensions within which parent-offspring relations are constructed. Having elaborated those themes, I shall review the consequences which follow from the various areas of social policy discussed in the book, before concluding with a discussion of the limits of policy intervention.

The dimensions of the parent-offspring relation

The overarching proposition of this book is that the duties parents owe to their children and the debts which children owe to their parents are socially constructed. The process of social construction is of course complex. The parent-offspring relation is in the first instance a biological or procreative relationship; it is none the less materially fashioned in historically specific circumstances; and the intrinsic meaning of the relationship is ideologically bounded. These three dimensions are analytically distinguishable, but they are closely interlocked in everyday experience.

Biology and procreative relations

The point has already been made in Chapter 1 that, though the respective roles of parents and children are socially defined, society itself defines such relationships in biological terms. The biological 'blood tie' has considerable symbolic and social significance. Kroll and Barrett (Chapter 4) point out that people have all sorts of complicated reasons for having children. It also emerges clearly from Ellis' and Thompson's chapters (Chapters 6 and 7) that people have all sorts of complicated reasons for feeling indebted to the parents who begot them. Fitches (Chapter 5) has reminded us, however, that the need to establish and to honour procreative relationships is culturally specific: the precise significance of the 'blood tie' is far from universal and its meaning may be more immediate and more compelling in some communities than in others.

On the one hand, having children may contribute to a sense of biological and social completeness: becoming a parent is for some people necessary to achieving adult status and identity. Upon the other hand, knowing the identity of one's biological parents and the hereditary basis of one's genetic makeup can be equally important for some people's sense of completeness and identity. What has emerged most consistently in preceding chapters is the way in which, in all cultures, the significance of social identity and responsibility is gendered; that is, it is socially constructed in relation to biological differences in sex. Though feminists like Fiona Williams (1989) have argued against crude biological reductionism, they also emphasise the importance of biology.

Understanding the significance of biology for parent-offspring relations is important, not only because there are ways in which biology inescapably defines and limits us, but also because human understanding makes it more and more possible to transcend or subvert biology. This has been especially significant in the case of the new reproductive technologies since, as Williams points out,

> Along with earlier developments in medical technology, like contraception and safe abortion, these offer women the possibility of greater control over their lives whilst they simultaneously expose them to the exercise of power by the medical profession who administer such technologies and the state which legislates upon the boundaries of their operation. (1989: 65)

Technologies which control fertility are capable of giving new significance to the socially constructed hierarchies of responsibility which attach to 'blood ties'. Not only is it now possible for people by choice to deprive themselves of children, it is also possible through *in vitro* fertilisation, donor insemination and surrogacy for people to beget children without themselves being fertile and/or without sexual union. Additionally, medical technology now has the capacity to produce 'designer babies', to allow prospective parents to select the sex and even other characteristics of their offspring. New reproductive technologies therefore raise new questions for the ontological basis of duties and responsibilities between parents and children; new moral and legal issues; and new questions about the extent to which the state should regulate the practices associated with 'artificial' parenthood (see, for example, Warnock 1984). As Stanworth has put it - 'By altering the boundaries between the biological and the social - by demanding human decision where previously there was biological destiny - the new technologies politicize issues concerning sexuality, reproduction, parenthood and family' (1987: 2).

These are issues which reach beyond the scope of this book. They are mentioned here, however, in order to underline the point that, though we cannot disengage ourselves from the biological parameters of our being, biology plays a subordinate role in determining social responsibilities. Medical professionals increasingly have the power to fashion procreative relationships at will. They also increasingly have the power to ensure the survival of infants and to extend the life of adults after procreation, potentially extending the duration of the relationships which parents and offspring can have with each other. However, it is policy makers who may claim the power to determine the responsibilities which shall pertain within such procreative relationships.

History and the political economy of procreation

Within pre-industrial societies the political economy of procreation was straightforward. Having children was a necessary process by which to provide the labour power upon which one's own future survival depended. Providing for one's parents was an obligation resulting from the general necessity of reciprocal human relations and the particular exigencies of intergenerational power. We have seen from Fitches' chapter (Chapter 5) that such considerations also apply in many contemporary Third World countries and may continue to influence the cultural beliefs of ethnic communities in countries like Britain.

What has emerged in other chapters, however, is that the political economy of procreation in Britain has been subject to major historical changes, such that children and aged parents have ceased to be economically constituted as assets, and have become 'burdens'. Childhood and old age are themselves socially constructed. The idea of childhood as a period of dependency between infancy and adulthood is of comparatively recent provenance (Gittins 1993; and see discussion in Chapter 1 above). The idea of 'old age' as a period of dependency and retirement from active labour is even more recent (Walker 1987). Townsend has suggested that, as longevity increases and labour markets tighten, expectations of retirement have been contrived as 'a kind of mass redundancy' (1991: 6).

In Chapter 2 I have drawn attention to the various factors which from the end of the nineteenth century have made children a financial burden upon their parents. The 'civilising' influence of protective legislation and compulsory education were to play a vital part in constituting modern childhood as a period of dependency. Berridge in Chapter 3 similarly points to the end of the nineteenth century as a time when new preoccupations with the welfare of children found legislative expression. Such legislation, however, was concerned merely to 'rescue' the children of the lower social orders and did not seek either to prescribe or to enforce the responsibilities of parents to their children.

In the twentieth century that has changed. Writers like Donzelot (1979) argue that a variety of medical, legal and policy interventions in western European jurisdictions have intersected in ways which secure the regulation of parental conduct. Whereas once, Donzelot claims, the family had itself constituted a form of government in which power was exercised by parents over children, it has now been reconstituted as an instrument of government through which professional and administrative power is exercised over parents and children alike.

Such a transition has been at times subtle, though in the sphere of youth justice - as Kroll and Barrett describe in Chapter 4 - it has sometimes been more explicit.

In the process, the political economy of procreation has become 'privatised' and inherently 'anti-social' (c.f. Barrett and McIntosh 1982). Child rearing is an especially private 'burden' which, as Eva Havas puts it, 'denies the notion that any child's disadvantage ultimately affects other children and the wider society. Thus each parent fights to obtain the best for their children .... viewing the gains of other children as taking from their own' (1995: 7). This shift may be finding new forms of expression in what Common in Chapter 8 calls the 'contractorisation' of state services: not only services for children, but services for vulnerable elderly people and the services which support adult offspring in caring for aged parents.

Ellis' and Thompson's chapters (Chapters 6 and 7) have illustrated the other side to the transition in the political economy of procreation. In the mid-nineteenth century average life expectancy in England was around 40 for men and 42 for women. In the late twentieth century it is 72 for men and 78 for women (Nissel 1987). What is more, the number of people in Britain aged 85 and over is projected to increase by half a million within the next 30 years (Kiernan and Wicks 1990). Our parents are more likely than before to survive into old age. Instead of this being seen in terms of new opportunities for inter-generational contact and support, it is seen in policy terms as problematic and in personal terms as burdensome.

The responsibilities which adult offspring have for their parents are not in symmetry with the responsibilities which parents have for their children. Whether there ever was a time of symmetry is at best uncertain, but Anderson (1971) claims there is a correlation between the degree of respect and attention which elderly people command in a society and the extent to which elderly people control resources in that society. The implication is that in industrialised capitalist societies procreative relationships will have become increasingly asymmetrical as power over resources has shifted to younger and more economically active generations. The evidence is that, in terms of their sense of normative obligation, people by and large give priority to their *immediate* 'family of procreation' (their spouses and children) above their 'family of orientation' (their parents and siblings) (Qureshi and Walker 1989). Caring for one's parents in their old age is likely therefore to be perceived as a greater imposition than caring for one's 'own' spouse or children in time of need. Responsibility within the procreative relationship tends, in other words, to be 'oriented' primarily in one direction.

Raising the visibility of 'informal' carers has drawn attention to the arduous nature of the (unpaid) work which adult children (primarily daughters) may none the less undertake for aged parents. At the same time, the ascendancy of New Right discourses that valorise self-sufficiency and individualism helps inform a perception that frail elderly and disabled parents who have not independently provided for their own care are an encumbrance. Ellis in Chapter 6 has demonstrated that the latest processes of community care needs assessment and service rationing implicitly incorporate a reworked version of the liable relatives provisions of the 1834 Poor Law. What has changed is that, while the occasions upon which it might have been necessary to 'persuade' a son or daughter to take in or provide for an aged parent would have been rare, now they are increasingly commonplace. Thompson in Chapter 7 similarly demonstrates how the social construction of the 'informal' or 'private' carer, though a recent phenomenon, is historically rooted in the patriarchal relations of the 'bourgeois family'. What has changed is not the gendered nature of the responsibilities which fall to daughters and sons, but the salience of those responsibilities and the difficulty in present economic and labour market conditions of meeting them.

Ideology and political dynamics

In Chapter 1 I contrasted the ideological positions of feminism and neo-conservative pro-familism: opposing positions which have each been developed with a significant degree of intellectual coherence. The political discourse of 'back to basics' which provided the backdrop to many of the recent policy reforms described in this book stems in one sense from a reaction against the former by the latter. However, the terms in which this is customarily expressed tend to be woefully simplistic. The scenario painted by British ministers is one in which an imagined golden age preceded the onset of the permissive 1960s and the 'trendy' left-wing and feminist intellectualism of the '70s. Thus Virginia Bottomley, Health Secretary and the government's appointed spokesperson on family matters, has declared

> It was in those same years that fashionable nostrums in education, housing and law and order took hold. Non-judgmental, permissive values undermined respect for the values of responsibility, community and self-help - the very values that families had honed and passed on down the centuries. It is in those years that we can trace the origins of so much extra family breakdown and the erosion of respect for law and order. (*Hansard*, Col. 449, 14 April 1994)

Such a view owes more to dogma than to historical analysis. It is true that since the 1960s family structure and attitudes have undergone a period of rapid change (Utting 1995) but the roots of such change lay in economic and social changes whose origins are much deeper than politicians suppose. The family has become an ideological totem, with each of the main political parties claiming to be 'the party of the family'. The Leader of the Labour Party, Tony Blair, has recently shifted his rhetoric onto the territory of 'back to basics', claiming - 'It is largely from family discipline that social discipline and a sense of responsibility are learnt. It is in the family that a sense of community is born.' (*Guardian* 30.3.95). Bottomley and Blair are equally immune to the thrust of the analysis by feminists such as Barrett and McIntosh (1982) who have contended that the essential individualism which underpins the ideology of the family is actually corrosive of community responsibility, since it elevates a competitive rather than a co-operative form of morality.

In the late 1980s and early 1990s, however, the political dynamics of the various reforms which have borne upon parents, children and their mutual responsibilities have been more subtle and complex than their associated political rhetoric might lead us to suspect. In Chapter 2 we saw that the Child Support Act, in spite of its ostensible origins in neo-conservative political thinking was able to attract support from both 'ethical' socialists and from some 'radical' feminists. Though the child support scheme entailed state intervention in private affairs, this provoked no resistance from neo-liberals and the libertarian Right. Though the scheme effectively 'privatised' elements of social security provision for lone-parents, it provoked little reaction from the traditional Left. The main opposition to the Act, though vociferous, was instrumentally rather than ideologically informed.

Berridge has argued in Chapter 3 that the 1989 Children Act was distinctive, not only because it attracted no ideological controversy, but because in many ways it embodied a progressive agenda which did not sit well with that of the government. Certainly, the Children Act sought to define the responsibilities rather than the rights of parents, but it also called for partnership between professionals and parents and a clear role for local authority social services departments. It may be that the government found child protection too sensitive an issue to politicise. Alternatively, they may have found it too difficult an issue around which to resolve the inherent tensions between the authoritarian/neo-conservative and libertarian/neo-liberal elements of New Right philosophy. Either way it appears that an agenda set largely by child care professionals and experts was allowed to proceed, as it were, by default. It can be seen from Kroll and Barrett's chapter (Chapter 4) that such inhibitions would not seem to have applied in the arena of youth justice policy, though the vacillation over policy detail which has been so evident during the 1980s and '90s is arguably attributable to the influence of competing authoritarian and libertarian Right wing tendencies.

Ellis, Thompson and Common, in Chapters 6, 7 and 8 respectively, have discussed various aspects of the distinctive ideological agenda which underpinned the community care provisions of the NHS and Community Care Act. Here was an explicit attempt to shift responsibilities from state to family. None the less, the state was to retain a role albeit as a funder and enabler of services and as broker in a quasi-market for social care.

The responsibilities imputed to parent-offspring relations therefore form but a part of a political discourse which is as concerned with selectively transforming the role of the state as it is with transferring responsibilities to families. Beneath the shallowness and inconsistency of political debate deeper ideological tensions remain. First, supporters of '*the* family' do not necessarily agree as to why the family as an ideological institution is to be valued: is it a bulwark against state interference and the insidious influence of administrative power (see, for example, Mount 1982); or is it a bulwark against the brutalising forces of competitive capitalism and 'a haven in a heartless world' (see, for example, Lasch 1977)? Second, critics of the relations of power which characterise the modern nuclear family may place stress upon quite different aspects of power: feminists upon the gendered basis of power relations within families; post-structuralists (and others) upon the institutional capacity of families to individuate, to accommodate and to discipline their members. 'The family' is a site of ideological controversy and struggle. Within families, however, parents continue in diverse ways to bear and to raise children, and in adulthood many of those children continue to sustain various kinds of supportive relationship with their parents.

Reference has been made by several of this volume's contributors to the work of Finch (1989b) and Finch and Mason (1993). That work has demonstrated that familial responsibilities are negotiated and sustained in spite rather than because of policy intervention. The quotidian nature of parent-offspring relations is worked through and changes over time. Such negotiations and change have a fundamental ideological significance, but the dynamics of political debate are only one of many influences upon the process.

The consequences of intervention

Given the complex and infinitely variable quality of parent-offspring relations the consequences of policy intervention are neither predictable, nor easy to interpret. Fitches in Chapter 5 has brought this most sharply into focus in the case of Britain's ethnic communities whose expectations of parent-offspring relations and of the role of the state may be at odds with those of policy makers and service providers. This opens up far reaching questions about the propriety of policy intervention and about the capacity of the state to define, still less impose, responsibilities. If none the less it is accepted that a welfare state should have a role in protecting vulnerable children and old people, and in supporting those who care for them, then it is important that the actual consequences of policy intervention should, so far as possible, be understood.

The earlier chapters in this book have discussed a range of recent legislative measures which bear upon the care, control or support of children and young people on the one hand (Child Support Act, Children Act and Criminal Justice Acts) and of frail elderly and disabled people on the other (the community care provisions of the NHS and Community Care Act). What has emerged is that, in certain respects, *some* of the consequences of that legislation may fall short or even run contrary to the intentions of policy makers. In concentrating in this section upon precisely those aspects of recent legislation, my intention is to explore where some of the limits of policy intervention may lie. My contention is that three kinds of perverse consequence can be described: consequences which go against the grain of popular aspirations; consequences which enhance rather than diminish administrative power; consequences which minimise or discourage responsibility.

The frustration of popular aspirations

My own and Katherine Ellis' chapters (Chapters 2 and 6 respectively) have illustrated how the child support and the community care schemes are each pushing against the tide of ordinary expectations in terms of how people would like to care for their children or their parents. There can be no doubting that, just as (almost) everybody is against sin, most people in white western European societies accept that mothers and (especially) fathers should support their children financially, and that it is right that sons and (especially) daughters should be prepared - if it is both possible and necessary - to care for their aged parents. In reality, however, people harbour a variety of expectations by which they would qualify or feel they are excused from such responsibilities. In neither case is the mere existence of a procreative relationship - a 'blood tie' - sufficient to guarantee the unconditional acceptance of responsibility.

In the case of child support, we have seen that the liability imposed by legislation can impinge, not only upon the relationship between 'qualifying children' and their 'absent parents', but also upon the relationship between 'estranged' parents, and sometimes too upon the relationship between 'absent parents' and the members of their 'second families'. The child support scheme has been introduced at a time when expectations of family relationships have been changing: when, on the one hand, the dissolution and reformation of households is more commonplace and when, on the other hand, the demand for emotionally satisfying relationships is more acute. When conjugal relationships break down, the very nature of the relationship between the separated partners - whether it be fragile, hostile or even violent - may represent an obstacle to the continuation of a satisfying relationship between a child of that partnership and the parent who has left. At the very least, the negotiation of a continued relationship between such a child and its non-custodial parent is likely to be delicate and easily disrupted. At the same time, if non-custodial parents establish new partnerships and thereby become step-parents, the immediacy of the relationships they develop with step-children may assume for them greater significance and represent a greater moral responsibility than that which they feel towards their biological child(ren).

The government's overriding objective in introducing the child support scheme was to reduce social security expenditure upon lone-parents and, indirectly, to provide symbolic support for the 'stable' two parent family. In the process, the legislation has privileged biological parenthood and elevated one kind of familial responsibility above others. It is this which threatens to frustrate the kind of satisfactions and associated responsibilities which many people seek from family relationships.

In the case of community care, we have seen that the processes by which responsibility for the care of a frail and elderly parent can be shifted in the direction of an adult daughter may generate a number of conflicts. On the part of the parent, especially mothers, such dependency may be unwelcome and threatening to her own identity since the care required can no longer be reciprocated. As argued above, reciprocity in inter-generational relations has become asymmetrical over time and parents by and large are and expect to be net givers of assistance to their children. It has been claimed that the living arrangements preferred by elderly people and their children in western European societies may be characterised by the phrase 'intimacy at a distance' (Rosenmayer and Kockeis 1963), and this in itself implies that the changes portended by the community care reforms require a significant cultural shift. In the event, the shift demanded may be greater than this, since the asymmetry of the intergenerational settlement often extends to an asymmetry of emotional attachments as well as to the direction in which material assistance has tended to flow. In the absence of mutual affection, caring relationships can be and often are held together by a sense of duty, but any move which imposes or which is seen as imposing such duties is not calculated to strengthen the bonds between adult offspring and their children.

The government has insisted that care in the community should, so far as possible, mean care by the community. There is however a growing body of evidence that public opinion is moving in favour of state/professional care within the community, rather than the kind of private/family care which the government seeks to promote (see, for example, Phillips 1992). The direction of social policy is such that, arguably, it is seeking to change the nature of the prevailing intergenerational settlement against the will and expectations of the people.

The propensity for disciplinary power

David Berridge's and Di Thompson's chapters (Chapters 3 and 7 respectively), while focusing upon two very different pieces of legislation, each draw attention to the subtler side of recent policy changes. The language of the Children Act when it speaks in terms of 'partnership' between parents and local authorities, and of the community care legislation when it speaks of choices by and support for carers, appears balanced and reassuring. In the context of prevailing relations of power, however, the language is capable of an alternative construction.

We have seen that the Children Act is a child- and family- centred piece of legislation which ostensibly did not so much transfer responsibility to parents from the state, as seek to 'enhance' parental responsibility. Parental responsibility was defined in a way which, quite unlike the Child Support Act, extends the concept so that it may apply to persons other than biological parents. To this extent, the Act is sensitive to the realities of contemporary expectations. In the case of children in need who are looked after by local authorities the Act provides, not that the responsibilities of parents should be overridden by the state, but that there should be a partnership between parents and social services. Certainly, this redresses the conspicuous imbalances of power between parents, children and the state which had applied under earlier legislation. We have seen however that the fears of some critics - that the resources necessary to make the Act fully effective might not be made available to local authorities - may well have been borne out. In particular, it had been foretold that a failure to implement the elements of preventative practice which the Act envisaged could create a climate in which it would be 'extremely difficult' to achieve a 'genuine partnership' between parents and local authorities (Harwin 1990: 93). While the Act may prove a highly effective instrument of child protection, it may 'founder on the attainment of its wider purposes of promoting child welfare by strengthening family bonds' (*ibid*: 95).

Though distancing himself from it, Berridge has helpfully drawn our attention to the work of Parton (1991) who has read certain ambiguities into the Children Act with regard to its potential for social regulation. From a Foucauldian perspective the notion of 'partnership' is significant. The implication is that, not only do parents have a responsibility from which they may not opt out, but that that responsibility will if necessary be exercised upon the terms set within an (unequal) partnership with a social services department. The language of 'partnership' implies voluntary submission to the competent authority of the state. When there is a crisis in the interdependent relations between parents and children, it is likely to be the state that defines what is in children's best interests and what parents' responsibilities might be. There is a sense in which the Children Act, because of its sophistication and sensitivity, holds the potential for extending rather than curtailing the reach of what Donzelot (1979) has called 'the tutelary complex'; that panoply of discreet interventions by which parental conduct may be regulated.

Returning for a moment to the community care legislation, we have seen that it achieved, in the course of its attenuated development in the 1980s and early '90s, a significant shift at the level of public discourse from a language which assumed the moral obligations of family members to a language which assumed the normality of private or 'informal' care. Thompson has demonstrated how the moral imperative to care has been socially reconstructed through managerialist discourse. Daughters and daughters-in-law who are drawn into providing care for an elderly or disabled person are constituted both as 'customers' of social services who have exercised an illusory choice and as 'service providers' within the mixed economy of care. The effect is disciplinary. The technical nature of contemporary community care robs the parent-offspring bond of its social and moral character by making it a requirement or technical feature of state policy.

The preclusion of reflexive responsibility

Brynna Kroll and David Barrett in Chapter 4 and Richard Common in Chapter 8 illustrate a rather different though equally perverse tendency in current policy reforms. Though one chapter focuses on youth justice reforms and the other upon the marketisation of social care, they each deal with reforms which explicitly limit the extent to which parents and children might reflect upon the nature of their mutual responsibilities. The hard-nosed discourses of law and order and market forces leave little room for notions of responsibility based upon human interdependency.

We have therefore seen that recent youth justice reforms, in seeking - sometimes literally - to place parents in the dock alongside their troublesome children, are concerned with 'understanding less and condemning more'. Here, implicitly, is a minimalist notion of parental responsibility which appeals to parental self-interest before the welfare of the child and which equates parental adequacy with the mere exercise of control.

Similarly, we have seen that the 'contractorisation' of social care may be associated with a minimalist notion of familial liability. In spite of the misty eyed romanticism with which prominent Conservatives recall a mythical age of self-sufficient communities and family values, the contract culture which they have promoted within education, health and social care is profoundly inimical to the kind of altruistic mutual responsibility upon which strong communities and caring families depend. When dependent frail elderly or disabled parents cannot be looked after by their adult children and there is no one else with whom to share such care, those who can pay may of course buy services directly. Those who cannot pay must now compete for a share of limited state funding controlled by social services departments who function, not only as assessors of need, but as rationers; not only as enablers, but as brokers in the marketplace for social care. The process is dehumanising in that it reduces the responsibilities which adult children may feel towards their parents, to a liability that is calculable, which should ideally be minimised, and which may be offloaded or contracted out. In place of the social negotiation of family responsibilities is a market negotiation.

Defining limits

1994 was the International Year of the Family. It was also the year in which, in Britain, an All Party Parliamentary Group on Parenting was established, albeit not as an official Committee of the House. The Group drew a number of conclusions bearing upon the need for better co-ordination between government departments and with health and local authorities; for better education and preventative work; for benefits reforms to lessen family poverty; for enhanced child care and 'family friendly' employment practices; for better support for carers; and it reiterated a call made in the 1970s by the Study Commission on the Family for 'Family Impact Statements' as a mechanism by which to ensure the future coherence of diverse kinds of policy intervention (APPG 1994). The Group did not, however, 'pursue the particular means through which general aspirations might be given effect' (Henwood 1995: 58) and, as Melanie Henwood has put it, the Group's suggestions and proposals offered 'not so much a policy agenda, as an agenda for further debate and refinement' (*ibid*: 64).

Also in 1994, the Commission for Social Justice produced its report, echoing several of the Parliamentary Group's suggestions, but calling more specifically for 'a clear legal statement of parental responsibilities [which] would help to underline a new commitment to children' (CSJ 1994: 320); and for 'a far fuller enquiry than we have been able to carry out ourselves' to develop options for a new form of social insurance to meet the costs of long-term social care for elderly and disabled people (*ibid*: 301). Once again, the call is tentative. It is a call for a debate about new beginnings.

If there is a will to fashion new policies, the contribution which this book seeks to make is to draw lessons from recent policy initiatives and to define some of the limits to which state intervention is or arguably should be subject. Emerging from the observations summarised in this chapter are three principal points.

First, it is clear that debts and duties cannot readily be imposed upon the parent-offspring relationship by the state. The nature of human interdependency is that mutual responsibilities must be socially negotiated. The imposition of duties is a form of exploitation; the imposition of debts, a form of usury.

Second, the integrity of parent-offspring relations can - often unobtrusively - be violated by forms of state intervention which have the power to specify and to supervise. The nature of the interdependency inherent to parent-offspring relations is such that it will often require support or facilitation through the mechanism of the state, but an endorsement of this principle should not obscure our awareness of disciplinary power.

Third, the duties and debts associated with the parent-offspring relationship are not calculable or founded in self-interest; they are fluid and founded in self-giving. This does not mean that such responsibilities are illusory or ineffectual, merely that they are by their nature reflexive and dependent for their existence upon some element of ontological meaning and mutual understanding.

We have additionally observed that parent-offspring relations are both highly gendered and culturally specific. Social policy clearly has a role, for example, in compensating those - especially women - upon whom debts and duties may fall disproportionately. However, social policy cannot compel people to adopt particular patterns of responsibility. Government may legitimately seek to promote certain kinds of responsibility, but it cannot do so by condemning human frailty as failure, by countermanding popular or cultural aspirations or beliefs, or by turning persuasion to coercion. The obligations which stem from the parent-offspring relation may be biologically, historically and ideologically determined, but they are neither absolute nor inescapable. There are all manner of ways in which parents and children care for each other and it is more important to assist them than it is to prescribe for them.

References

Adcock, M. and White, R. (1985) *Good-enough parenting*, British Agencies for Adoption and Fostering, London.

Adler, B. (1994) 'Detention' *The Guardian*, 26 August.

Ahmed, W. (ed.) (1993) *'Race' and Health in Contemporary Britain*, Open University Press, Buckingham.

Aldgate, J., Tunstill, J. and McBeath, G. (1993) *Highlights from a National Study of the Implementation of Section 17 of the Children Act 1989 in England.* University of Leicester School of Social Work, Leicester.

Aldgate, J., Tunstill, J. and McBeath, G. (1994) *Implementing Section 17 of the Children Act - the first 18 months.* A report for the DoH, Leicester University.

All Party Parliamentary Group (APPG) (1994) *Report of the All Party Parliamentary Group on Parenting and International Year of the Family UK*, Parliamentary Hearings, HMSO, London.

Allen, I., Hogg, D. and Peace, S. (1992) *Elderly People: Choice, Participation and Satisfaction*, Policy Studies Institute, London.

Ames, J. (1991) *Just Deserts or Just Growing Up?* National Children's Bureau, London.

Anderson, E. and Morgan, A. (1987) *Provision for Children in Need of Boarding/Residential Education*, Boarding Schools Association, Durham.

Anderson, M. (1971) *Family Structure in Nineteenth Century Lancashire*, Cambridge University Press, Cambridge.

Arber, S. and Ginn, J. (1991) 'Gender, class and income inequalities in later life', *British Journal of Sociology*, Vol. 42 No. 3.

Aslam, M. and Healy, A. (1989) *The Asian Community: Medicine and Traditions,* Silver Link Publishing, Nottingham.

Athwall, W. (1990) 'A special case for special treatment', *Social Work Today*, February.

Audit Commission (1986) *Making a Reality of Community Care: A report*, HMSO, London.

Audit Commission (1992) *Community Care: Managing the Cascade of Change*, HMSO, London.
Baines, C. Evans, P. and Neysmith, S. (eds.) (1991) *Women's Caring. Feminist Perspectives on Social Welfare*, McClelland & Stewart, Toronto.
Baldock, J. and Ungerson, C. (1991) 'What d'ya want if you don' want money? - a feminist critique of "paid volunteering"', in Maclean, M. and Groves, D. (eds.) *Women's Issues in Social Policy*, Routledge, London.
Baldwin, S. and Parker, G. (1989) 'The Griffiths Report on Community Care' in Brenton, M. and Ungerson, C. (eds.) *Social Policy Review 1988/89*, Longman/Social Policy Association, Harlow.
Bamford, T. (1990) *The Future of Social Work*, Macmillan, Basingstoke.
Barclay, P. (1995) *Joseph Rowntree Foundation Inquiry into Income and Wealth*, Vol.1, Joseph Rowntree Foundation, York.
Barrett, M. and McIntosh, M. (1982) *The Anti-social Family*, Verso, London.
Bayley, M. (1973) *Mental Handicap and Community Care: a Study of Mentally Handicapped People in Sheffield*, Routledge & Kegan Paul, London.
Bebbington, A. and Miles, J. (1989) 'The background of children who enter local authority care', *British Journal of Social Work*, Vol. 19 pp 349-368.
Becker, S. (ed.) (1991) *Windows of Opportunity*, Child Poverty Action Group, London.
Begum, N. (1990) *Burden of gratitude: Women with disabilities receiving personal care*, Social Care Practice Centre/Department of Applied Social Studies, University of Warwick.
Begum, N. (1992) 'Disabled Women and the Feminist Agenda', in Hinds, H., Phoenix, A., and Stacey, J. (eds.) *Working Out, New Directions for Women's Studies*, Falmer Press, Brighton.
Bennett, F. and Chapman, V. (1990) *The Poverty of Maintenance*, Child Poverty Action Group, London.
Berger, P. and Berger, B. (1983) *The War Over the Family*, Hutchinson, London.
Berman, P., Hunter, D. and McMahon, L. (1990) 'Keep It Integrated' *Health Service Journal*, Vol. 5 pp. 996-997
Berridge, D. (1994) 'Foster and residential care reassessed: a research perspective', *Children and Society*, Vol.8 No. 2.

Biehal, N., Clayden, J., Stein, M. and Wade, J. (1992) *Prepared for Living? A Survey of People Leaving the Care of Three Local Authorities*, National Children's Bureau, London.

Blaxter, M. (1980) *The Meaning of Disability*, Heinemann, London.

Bond, J. (1992) 'The Politics of Caregiving: The Professionalisation of Informal Care', *Ageing and Society*, Vol. 12 pp. 5-21

Bottomley, V. (1994) 'The Government and Family Policy: Background Note' in *Report of the All Party Parliamentary Group on Parenting and International Year of the Family UK*, Parliamentary Hearings, HMSO, London.

Bowen Thomas, Sir Ben (1968) 'The debt to my parents' in *By Request: from 'Ten to Eight'* on Radio 4, BBC Publications, London.

Bradshaw, J. and Holmes, H. (1989) *Living on the Edge: a Study of the Living Standards of Families on Benefit in Tyne & Wear*, Tyneside Child Poverty Action Group, CPAG, London.

Bradshaw, J. and Millar, J. (1991) *Lone Parent Families in the UK*, DSS Research Report No. 6, HMSO, London.

Brindle, D. (1988) 'Ministerial foot in the mental hospital door' *The Guardian*, 19 August

Broadhurst, P. (1963) *The Science of Animal Behaviour*, Penguin, Harmondsworth.

Brown, H. and Smith, H. (1993) 'Women Caring For People: the mismatch between rhetoric and reality?', *Policy and Politics*, Vol. 21 No. 3.

Brown, J. (1992) 'Which way for the family: choices for the 1990s' in Manning, N. and Page, R. (eds.) *Social Policy Review 4,* Social Policy Association, Canterbury.

Bullock, R., Little, M. and Millham, S. (1993) *Going Home. The Return of Children Separated from their Families*, Dartmouth, Aldershot.

Bulmer, M. (1987) *The Social Basis of Community Care*, Unwin Hyman, London.

Burghes, L. (1993) *One-parent families: Policy Options for the 1990s*, Family Policy Studies Centre/Joseph Rowntree Foundation, York.

Burke, B. and Dalrymple, J. (1991) 'Implementing Race and Culture issues using the Children Act 1989', *Panel News*, September 1991, pp.4-8.

Carabine, J. (1992) 'Constructing women: women's sexuality and social policy', *Critical Social Policy*, Issue 34.

Cavadino, M. (1994) 'Persistent Young Offenders', *Journal of Child Law*, Vol. 6 No. 1.

Cavadino, M. and Dignan, J. (1992) 'From System Disaster to Systems Management' in Cavadino, M. and Dignan, J. (eds.) *The Penal System: An Introduction*, Sage, London.

Cheetham, J. (1993) 'Social work and community care in the 1990's: pitfalls and potential', Page, R. and Baldock, J. (eds.) *Social Policy Review 5*, Social Policy Association, Canterbury.

Child Support Agency (CSA) (1994) *Child Support Agency: the first two years* - annual report 1993/4 and business plan 1994/5, CSA 2066.

Chodorow, N. (1978) *The Reproduction of Mothering: Psychoanalysis and the Sociology of Gender*, California University Press, Berkeley.

Clarke, J., Cochrane, A., and McLaughlin, E. (eds.) (1994) *Managing Social Policy*, Sage, London.

Clarke, K., Craig, G. and Glendinning, C. (1993) *Children Come First? The Child Support Act and Lone-Families: a Research Project*, The Children's Society, London.

Clarke, K., Glendinning, C. and Craig, G. (1994) *Losing Support: Children and the Child Support Act*, The Children's Society, London.

Clarke, L. (1989) *Children's Changing Circumstances: Recent Trends and Future Prospects*, Centre for Population Studies, London School of Hygiene and Tropical Medicine, London.

Clode, D., Parker, C. and Etherington, S. (eds.) (1987) *Towards the Sensitive Bureaucracy*, Gower, Aldershot.

Cochrane, A. (1993) *Whatever Happened to Local Government?* Open University Press, Buckingham.

Coleman, J. and Warren-Adamson, C. (eds) (1992) *Youth Policy in the 1990s*, Routledge, London.

Commission on Social Justice (CSJ) (1994) *Social Justice: Strategies for National Renewal*, Vintage, London.

Common, R. (1993) 'Contracting Out Social Services: Some Lessons from the United States', *Local Economy Quarterly* , Vol. 2 No. 1.

Common, R. and Flynn, N. (1992) *Contracting for Care*, Joseph Rowntree Foundation, York.

Cooper, A. *et al* (1995) *Positive Child Protection: A View From Abroad*, Russell House, Lyme Regis.

Cooper, D. (1972) *The Death of the Family*, Penguin, Harmondsworth.

Cotton, M. and Hellinckx, W. (1994) 'Residential and Foster Care in the European Community', *British Journal of Social Work* , Vol. 24 No. 5.

Crisp, A. (1994) 'Children First', *Community Care*, Inside Series on Youth Crime, 28 July.

Crook, F. (1994) 'Man enough', *Community Care*, Inside Series on Youth Crime, 28 July.

Currer, C. and Stacey, M. (1991) *Concepts of Health and Illness*, Berg Publications, New York and Oxford.

Daatland, S. (1990) ''What are Families For?' On Family Solidarity and Preference for Help', *Ageing and Society*, Vol. 10 pp. 1-15

Dale, J. and Foster, P. (1986) *Feminists and State Welfare*, Routledge & Kegan Paul, London.

Dalley, G. (1988) *Ideologies of Caring: Rethinking Community and Collectivism*, Macmillan, Basingstoke.

Dalley, G. (1993) 'Caring: a legitimate interest of older women', in Bernard, M. and Meade, K. (eds.) *Women Come of Age*, Edward Arnold, London.

Davies, A. and Edwards, K. (1990) *Twelve Charity Contracts* , Directory of Social Change, London.

Dean, H. (1991) *Social Security and Social Control*, Routledge, London.

Dean, H. (1993) 'Social Security: the Income Maintenance Business' in Taylor-Gooby, P. and Lawson, R. (eds.) *Markets and Managers: New Issues in the Delivery of Welfare*, Open University Press, Buckingham.

Dean, H. and Taylor-Gooby, P. (1992) *Dependency Culture: the Explosion of a Myth*, Harvester Wheatsheaf, Hemel Hempstead.

Dennis, N. and Erdos, G. (1993) *Families Without Fatherhood*, second edition, Institute of Economic Affairs, London.

Department of Health (DoH) (1989) *An Introduction to the Children Act: A new framework for the care and upbringing of children*, HMSO, London.

Department of Health (DoH) (1990) *Community Care In the Next Decade And Beyond*, HMSO, London.

Department of Health (DoH) (1992) *The Children Act of 1989: Child Protection Guidance for Senior Nurses, Health Visitors and Midwives,* HMSO, London.

Department of Health (DoH) (1993) *Children in Care in England and Wales, March 1991*, Department of Health, London.

Department of Health and Department of Social Security (DoH/DSS) (1989) *Caring for People: Community Care in the Next Decade and Beyond*, Cm. 849, HMSO, London.

Department of Health and Social Security (DHSS) (1971) *Better Services for the Mentally Handicapped*, Cmnd. 4683, HMSO, London.

Department of Health and Social Security (DHSS) (1975) *Better Services for the Mentally Ill*, Cmnd. 6233, HMSO, London.
Department of Health and Social Security (DHSS) (1976) *Priorities for Health and Personal Social Services in England*, HMSO, London.
Department of Health and Social Security (DHSS) (1978) *A Happier Old Age*, HMSO, London.
Department of Health and Social Security (DHSS) (1981) *Growing Older*, Cmnd. 8173, HMSO, London.
Department of Health and Social Security (DHSS) (1985a) *Review of Child Care Law: Report to Ministers of an Inter-departmental Working Party*. HMSO, London.
Department of Health and Social Security (DHSS) (1985b) *Social Work Decisions in Child Care: Recent Research Findings and their Implications*. HMSO, London.
Department of Health and Welsh Office (1994) *Children Act Report 1993*, HMSO, London.
Department of Health Social Services Inspectorate (1991) *Purchase of Service*, HMSO, London.
Department of Social Security (DSS) (1990) *Children Come First*, Cm.1264, two volumes, HMSO, London.
Department of Social Security (DSS) (1995) *Improving Child Support*, Cm.2745, HMSO, London.
Dominelli, L. and McLeod, E. (1989) *Feminist Social Work*, Macmillan, Basingstoke.
Donzelot, J. (1979) *The Policing of Families*, Hutchinson, London.
Dyer, C. and Bell, A. (1994) 'Call of the Wild', *The Guardian*, 26 July.
Eastman, M. (1984) *Old Age Abuse,* Age Concern England, London.
Eisenstein, H. (1984) *Contemporary Feminist Thought*, Allen & Unwin, London.
Ellis, J. (1975) 'Differing conceptions of a child's needs: Some implications for Social Work with West African children and their parents', *British Journal of Social Work*, Vol. 7 No. 2.
Ellis, K. (1993) *Squaring the Circle: User and carer participation in needs assessment*, Joseph Rowntree Foundation/Community Care, York.
Equal Opportunities Commission (1980) *The Experience of Caring for Elderly and Handicapped Dependants: Survey Report*, Equal Opportunities Commission, Manchester.
Evandrou, M., Arber, S., Dale, A., and Gilber, G. N. (1989) 'Who cares for the elderly? Family care, provision and receipt of statutory service', in Philipson, C., Bernard, M., and Strang, P. (eds.)

Dependency and Interdependency in Old Age: Theoretical Perspectives and Policy Alternatives, Croom Helm, London.

Evandrou, M., Falkingham, J., and Glennerster, H. (1991) 'The Personal Social Services: Everyone's Poor Relation but Nobody's Baby', in Hills, J. (ed.) *The State of Welfare. The Welfare State in Britain since 1974*, Clarendon, Oxford.

Falkingham, J. and Victor, C. (1991) 'The Myth of the Woopie?: Incomes, the Elderly, and Targeting Welfare', *Ageing and Society*, Vol. 11 pp. 471-93

Ferris, J. (1991) 'Green Politics and the Future of Welfare' in Manning, N. (ed.) *Social Policy Review 1990-91*, Longman, Harlow.

Finch, J. (1989a) 'Social policy, social engineering and the family in the 1990s' in Bulmer, M., Lewis, J. and Piachaud, D. (eds.) *The Goals of Social Policy,* Unwin Hyman, London.

Finch, J. (1989b) *Family Obligations and Social Change*, Polity Press, Cambridge.

Finch, J. and Groves, D. (1980) 'Community care and the family: a case for equal opportunities?', *Journal of Social Policy*, Vol. 9 No. 4.

Finch, J. and Mason, J. (1990) 'Filial Obligations and Kin Support for Elderly People', *Ageing and Society,* Vo. 10 pp. 151-175

Finch, J. and Mason, J. (1992) *Negotiating Family Responsibilities*, Routledge, London.

Finch, J. and Mason, J. (1993) *Negotiating Family Responsibilities*, Routledge, London.

Fisher, M., Marsh, P. and Phillips, D. with Sainsbury, E. (1986) *In and Out of Care: The Experiences of Children, Parents and Social Workers*, Batsford, London.

Fitches, R. (1994) 'Disability in the Bengali community', *Children U.K.*, Issue 1, Summer, National Children's Bureau, London.

Flynn, N. and Hurley, D. (1993) *The Market For Care*, Public Sector Management, London School of Economics and Political Science, London.

Foster, P. (1991) 'Residential care of frail elderly people: a positive re-assessment' *Social Policy and Administration*, Vol. 25 No. 2.

Fox Harding, L. (1991) *Perspectives in Child Care Policy*, Longman, Harlow.

Fox, R. (1967) *Kinship and Marriage*, Penguin, Hamondsworth.

Franklin, B. (ed.) (1986) *The Rights of Children*, Blackwell, Oxford.

Freeman, M. (1983a) 'Freedom and the welfare state: Child-rearing, parental autonomy and state intervention', *Journal of Social Welfare Law*, March.

Freeman, M. (1983b) 'The Concept of children's rights', in Geach, H. and Szwed, E. (eds.) *Providing Civil Justice for Children*, Edward Arnold, London.
Freeman, M. (1983c) *The Rights and Wrongs of Children.* Frances Pinter, London.
Freeman, M. (1992) *Children, Their Families and the Law*, Macmillan, Basingstoke.
Frost, N. and Stein, M. (1989) *The Politics of Child Welfare: Inequality, Power and Change*, Harvester/Wheatsheaf, Hemel Hempstead.
Gamble, A. (1988) *The Free Market and the Strong State: the Politics of Thatcherism*, Macmillan, Basingstoke.
Garnett, L. (1992) *Leaving Care and After*, National Children's Bureau. London.
Garnham, A. and Knights, E. (1994a) *Child Support Handbook*, second edition 1994/95, Child Poverty Action Group, London.
Garnham, A. and Knights, E. (1994b) *Putting the Treasury First: the Truth about Child Support*, Child Poverty Action Group, London.
George, L. and Maddox, G. (1989) 'Social and behavioral aspects of institutional care' in Ory, M. and Bond, K. (eds.) *Ageing and Health Care*, Routledge, London.
George, V. and Wilding, P. (1984) *The Impact of Social Policy*, Routledge & Kegan Paul, London.
George, V. and Wilding, P. (1985) *Ideology and Social Welfare*, Routledge & Kegan Paul, London.
Gibbs, I. (1991) 'Income, Capital and the Cost of Care in Old Age', *Ageing and Society*, Vol. 11, pp. 373-97
Gilligan, C. (1982) *In a Different Voice: Psychological Theory and Women's Development*, Harvard University Press, Cambridge, Mass.
Gittins, D. (1993) *The Family in Question: Changing Households and Familiar Ideologies*, second edition, Macmillan, Basingstoke.
Glaser, B. and Strauss, A. (1967) *The Discovery of Grounded Theory*, Aldine De Gruyter, New York.
Glendinning, C. (1983) *Unshared Care: Parents and their disabled children*, Routledge, London.
Glendinning, C. (1985) *A Single Door*, George Allen & Unwin, London.
Glendinning, C. and Millar, J. (eds.) (1992) *Women and Poverty in Britain the 1990s*, Harvester Wheatsheaf, Hemel Hempstead.
Golding P. and Middleton, S. (1982) *Images of Welfare: Press and Public Attitudes to Poverty*, Martin Robertson, Oxford.

Goldstein, J., Freud, A. and Solnit, A. (1973) *Beyond the Best Interests of the Child*, Free Press, New York.

Goldstein, J., Freud, A. and Solnit, A. (1980) *Before the Best Interests of the Child*. Burnett Books/André Deutsch.

Gough, K. (1975) 'On the Origin of the Family', *Journal of Marriage and the Family*, 33 (cited in Morgan, D. *Social Theory and the Family*, Routledge & Kegan Paul, London).

Graham, H. (1983) 'Caring: A Labour of Love', in Finch, J. and Groves, D. (eds.) *A Labour of Love: Women, Work and Caring*, Routledge & Kegan Paul, London.

Graham, H. (1991) 'The Concept of Caring in Feminist Research: The Case of Domestic Service', *Sociology*, Vol. 25 No. 1.

Graham, H. (1993a) 'Feminist Perspectives on Caring' in Bornat, J., Pereira, C., Pilgrim, D. & Williams F. (eds.) *Community Care: A Reader*, Macmillan/Open University, Basingstoke.

Graham, H. (1993b) 'Social Divisions in Caring', *Women's Studies International Forum*, Vol. 16 No. 5.

Gray, A. and Jenkins, B. (1993) 'Markets, managers and the public service: The changing of a culture', in Taylor-Gooby, P.and Lawson, R. (eds.) *Markets and Managers. New Issues in the Delivery of Welfare*, Open University Press, Buckingham.

Green, D. (1991) 'Liberty, Poverty and the Underclass: a Classical-Liberal Approach to Public Policy', paper to a conference, *The Idea of an Underclass in Britain*, Policy Studies Institute, London, 26 February.

Griffiths, Sir Roy (1988) *Community Care: Agenda for Action. A Report to the Secretary of State for Social Services*, HMSO, London.

Hagell, A. and Newburn, T. (1994) *Persistent Young Offenders*, Policy Studies Institute, London.

Hake, J. (1972) *Child rearing practices in Northen Nigeria*, Ibadan University Press.

Hale, Sir Matthew (1683) *A Discourse Touching Provision for the Poor*, William Shrowsbery, London.

Hall, S. *et al* (1978) *Policing the Crisis: Mugging, the State, Law and Order*, Macmillan, Basingstoke.

Hallett, C. (1989) *Women and Social Services Departments*, Harvester Wheatsheaf, Hemel Hempstead.

Halsey, A.H. (1993) 'Changes in the Family', *Children and Society*, Vol.7 No.2

Hanmer, J. and Statham, (1988) *Women and Social Work. Towards a Woman-Centred Practice*, Macmillan, Basingstoke.

Hantrias, L. (1994) 'Comparing Family Policy in Britain, France and Germany', *Journal of Social Policy*, Vol. 23 No. 2.

Harding, T. (ed.) (1992) *Great Expectations .... and Spending on Social Services*, Social Services Policy Forum Paper No. 1, National Institute for Social Work, London.

Harkness, S., Machin, S. and Waldfogel, J. (1994) 'Women's pay and family income inequality' in *Findings*, Social Policy Research 60: Joseph Rowntree Foundation, York.

Harris, R. (1985) 'Towards Just Welfare: A Consideration of Current Controversy in the Theory of Juvenile Justice' in *British Journal of Criminology*, Vol. 25, No.1.

Harwin, J. (1990) 'Parental reponsibilities in the Children Act 1989' in Manning, N. and Ungerson, C. (eds.) *Social Policy Review 1989-90,* Longman/Social Policy Association, Harlow.

Havas, E. (1995) 'The Family as Ideology', *Social Policy and Administration*, Vol. 29 No. 1.

Hearn, J. and Parkin, W. (1987) *'Sex at Work': the power and paradox of organisation sexuality*, Harvester Wheatsheaf, Hemel Hempstead.

Helman, C. (1991) *Culture, Health and Illness*, Wright, Kent.

Henley, A. (1979) *Asians in Britain: Caring for Muslims and their families. Religious aspects of care*, DHSS/Kings Fund, London.

Henwood, M. (1992) 'Demographic and family change', in Harding, T. (ed.) *Who Owns Welfare? Questions on the social services agenda*, Social Services Policy Forum, National Institute for Social Work, London.

Henwood, M. (1995) 'Family Policy: Retrospect and Prospect', *Social Policy and Administration*, Vol. 29 No. 1.

Henwood, M., Jowell, T. and Wistow, G. (1991) *All things come (to those who wait?)*, King's Fund Institute, London.

Hewitt, P. (1993) *About Time: the Revolution in Work and Family Life*, Rivers Oram, London.

Hills, J. (1995), *Joseph Rowntree Foundation Inquiry into Income and Wealth*, Vol. 2 'A summary of the evidence' Joseph Rowntree Foundation, York.

Hoggett, B. and Pearl, D. (1991) *The Family, Law and Society*, third edition, Butterworth, London.

Hoggett, P. and Taylor, M. (1993) 'Quasi Markets and the Transformation of the Independent Sector, paper prepared for *Quasi-markets: The Emerging Findings*, 22-24 March, School for Advanced Urban Studies, Bristol.

Holman, B. (1988) *Putting Families First: Prevention and Child Care*, Macmillan, Basingstoke.

Holman, R. (1973) *Trading in children*, Routledge and Kegan Paul, London.
Holman, R. (1976) *Inequality in Child Care*, Child Poverty Action Group, London.
Holt, J. (1975) *Escape from Childhood. The Needs and Rights of Children*, Penguin, Harmondsworth.
Home Office (1980) *Young Offenders*, HMSO, London.
Home Office, Department of Health, Department of Education and Science and Welsh Office (1991) *Working Together Under the Children Act 1989. A Guide to Arrangements for Inter-agency Co-operation for the Protection of Children from Abuse*, HMSO, London.
Hood, C. (1991) A Public Management for all Seasons? *Public Administration*, Vol.69 No. 1.
Hornby, S (1993) *Collaborative Care*, Blackwell, Oxford.
House of Commons Social Services Committee (1984) *Second Report from the Social Services Committee (Session 1983-4) Children in Care (The Short Report)*, HMSO, London.
Howard, M. (1993) Speech to Conservative Party Conference, Autumn.
Hudson, H. (1993) 'Needs-led assessment: Nice idea shame about the reality?', *Health and Social Care in the Community*, Vol. 1 No. 2.
Hughes, B. and Mtezuka, M. (1992) 'Social work and older women: where have older women gone?', in Langan, M. and Day, L. (eds.)*Women, Oppression and Social Work. Issues in Anti-Discriminatory Practice*, Routledge, London.
Hugman, R. (1994) 'Social Work and Case Management in the UK: Models of Professionalism and Elderly People', *Ageing and Society*, Vol. 14 pp. 237-53.
Ingleby Report (1960) *Report of the Committee on Children and Young Persons*, HMSO, London.
Johnson, P. and Falkingham, J. (1992) *Ageing and Economic Welfare*, Sage, London.
Jones J (1993) 'Care in the Community' *The Independent on Sunday*, 10 January .
Joshi, H. (1992) 'The Cost of Caring' in Glendinning, C. and Millar, J. (eds.) *Women and Poverty in Britain: the 1990s*, Harvester Wheatsheaf, Hemel Hempstead.
Kardiner, A. (1981) *Clinical Anthropology: A Contemporary Perspective*, second edition, Keesing, Holt Rinehart and Winston, London.
Keith, L. (1992) 'Who Cares Wins? Women, Caring and Disability', *Disability, Handicap and Society*, Vol. 7 No. 2.

Kellmer Pringle, M. (1974) *The Needs of Children*, Hutchinson, London.
Kiernan, K. (1992) 'Men and Women at Work and at Home' in Jowell, R., Brook, L., Prior, G. and Taylor, B. (eds.) *British Social Attitudes: the Ninth Report*, Gower/SCPR, Aldershot.
Kiernan, K. and Wicks, M. (1990) *Family change and future policy*, Joseph Rowntree Foundation/Family Policy Studies Centre, York.
King's Fund Centre/Nuffield Institute (1994) *Fit for Change?* King's Fund Centre, London.
Kleinman, A. (1980) *Patients and Healers in the Context of Culture*, University of California Press, Berkley.
Kumar, V. (1993) *Poverty and Inequality in the UK: The Effects on Children*, National Children's Bureau, London.
Labour Party (1992) *Its Time to Get Britain Working Again*, election manifesto, Labour Party, London.
Laing, R.D. (1971) *The Family and Other Essays*, Tavistock, London.
Land, H. (1975) 'The Introduction of Family Allowances' in Hall, R., Land, H., Parker, R. and Webb, A. *Change, Choice and Conflict in Social Policy,* Heinnemann, London.
Land, H. (1991) 'Time to Care', in MacLean, M. and Groves, D. (eds.) *Women's Issues in Social Policy*, Routledge, London.
Land, H. and Rose, H. (1985) 'Compulsory Altruism for Some or an Altruistic Society for All?' in Bean, P., Ferris, J. and Whynes, D. (eds.) *In Defence of Welfare*, Tavistock, London.
Langan, M. (1990) 'Community care in the 1990s: the community care White Paper: "Caring for People"', *Critical Social Policy*, Vol. 10 No. 2.
Langan, M. and Clarke, J. (1994) 'Managing in the Mixed Economy of Care', in Clarke, J., Cochrane, A. and McLaughlin, E. (eds.) *Managing Social Policy*, Sage, London.
Langan, M. and Day, L. (1992) *Women, Oppression and Social Work. Issues in Anti-Discriminatory Practice,* Routledge, London.
Lasch, C. (1977) *Haven in a Heartless World: the Family Besieged*, Basic Books, New York.
Laslett, P. (1972) 'The History of the Family' in Laslett, L. and Wall, R. (eds.) *Household and Family in Past Time*, Cambridge University Press, Cambridge.
Lawson, R. (1993) 'The new technology of management in the personal social services', in Taylor-Gooby, P. and Lawson, R. (eds.) *Markets and Managers. New Issues in the Delivery of Welfare*, Open University Press, Buckingham.

Lerman, P. (1982) *Deinstitutionalization and the Welfare State*, Rutgers University Press, New Brunswick, NJ.

Levy, A. (1994) 'The end of childhood', *The Guardian*, 29 November.

Lewis, J. and Meredith, B. (1988) *Daughters who Care: Daughters caring for mothers at home*, Routledge, London.

Lipsky, M. (1980) *Street-level Bureaucracy*, Russell Sage, New York.

Lister, R. (1990) 'Women, Economic Dependency and Citizenship' *Journal of Social Policy*, Vol.19 No.4.

Maclean, M. and Eekelaar, J. (1993) 'Child Support: the British Solution' *International Journal of Law and the Family*, Vol.7 No.2.

Malthus, T. (1798) *Essay on the Principle of Population as it Affects the Future Improvement of Society*, Johnson, London.

Marchant, C. (1993) 'Family Values', *Community Care*, 13 May.

Marshall, A. (1890) *Principles of Economics* (cited in George, V. and Wilding, P. (1984) *The Impact of Social Policy*, Routledge & Kegan Paul, London.)

McGlone F. and Cronin N. (1994) *A Crisis in Care? The future of family and state care for older people in the European Union*. Family Policy Studies Centre, London.

Millar, J. (1992) 'Lone Mothers and Poverty' in Glendinning, C. and Millar, J. (eds.) *Women and Poverty in Britain: the 1990s*, Harvester Wheatsheaf, Hemel Hempstead.

Millar, J. (1993) 'Foreword' to Garnham, A. and Knights, E. *Child Support Handbook*, first edition 1993/94, Child Poverty Action Group, London.

Millar, J. (1994) 'Poor Mothers and Absent Fathers: Support for Lone Parents in Comparative Perspective', paper given to Social Policy Association Conference, *Families in Question*, University of Liverpool, 12-14, July.

Miller, A. (1987) *The Drama of being a Child*, Virago Press, London.

Millham, S., Bullock, R., Hosie, K. and Haak, M. (1985) *Lost in Care. The Problems of Maintaining Links Between Children in Care and their Families*, Gower, Aldershot.

Mills, C. Wright (1959) *The Sociological Imagination*, Penguin, Harmondsworth.

Modood, T. (1994) *Racial Equality: Colour, Culture and Justice*, Commission on Social Justice Issue Paper No. 5, Institute for Public Policy Research, London.

Moore, J. (1987) *Welfare and Dependency*, speech to Conservative Party Constituencies' Association, September.

Morris, A., Giller, H., Szwed, E. and Geach, H. (1980) *Justice for Children*, Macmillan, Basingstoke.
Morris, J. (1991) '"Us" and "Them"? Feminist research, community care and disability', *Critical Social Policy*, Vol. 11 No. 3.
Morris, J. (1992) 'Personal and Political: a feminist perspective on researching physical disability', *Disability, Handicap and Society*, Vol. 7 No. 2.
Morris, J. (1993a) *Independent Lives? Community care and disabled people*, Macmillan, Basingstoke.
Morris, J. (1993b) 'Key Task 1 Criteria Motives', *Community Care*
Morris, S and Wasoff, F. (1994) 'The Child Support Act: a Victory for Women?', paper given to Social Policy Association Conference, *Families in Question*, University of Liverpool, 12-14 July.
Moser, C. (1989) 'The social construction of dependency: comments from a Third World perspective' in Bulmer, M., Lewis, J. and Piachaud, D. (eds.) *The Goals of Social Policy*, Unwin Hyman, London.
Mount, F. (1982) *The Subversive Family*, Jonathan Cape, London.
Murray, C. (1984) *Losing Ground: American Social Policy 1950-1980*, Basic Books, New York
Murray, C. (1990) *The Emerging British Underclass*, Institute of Economic Affairs, London
National Association for the Care and Resettlement of Offenders (NACRO) (1993) *Community Provision for Young People in the Youth Justice System*, NACRO, London.
National Association of Citizens' Advice Bureaux (NACAB) (1994) *Child Support: One Year On*, NACAB, London.
National Council for One Parent Families (NCOPF) (1994) *The Child Support Agency's First Year: the Lone Parent Case*, NCOPF, London.
Newman, J. and Clarke, J. (1994) 'Going about Our Business? The Managerialisation of Public Services', in Clarke, J., Cochrane, A. and McLaughlin, E. (eds.) *Managing Social Policy*, Sage, London.
Nissel, M. (1987) *People Count*, Office of Population Censuses and Surveys, HMSO, London.
Nissel, M. and Bonnerjea, L. (1982) *Family Care of the Handicapped Elderly: Who Pays?*, Policy Studies Institute, London.
Nocon, A. (1994) *Collaboration in Community Care in the 1990s*, Business Education, Sunderland.
Normann, R. (1991) *Service Management*, second edition, John Wiley and Sons, Chichester.
Novak, M. *et al.* (1987) *The New Consensus on Family and Welfare*, American Enterprise Institute, Washington.

O'Higgins, M. (1984) 'Privatisation and Social Security', *Political Quarterly*, Vol.55 No.2.

Office of Population Censuses and Surveys (OPCS) (1987) *General Household Survey 1985*, HMSO, London.

Oliver, M. (1990) *The Politics of Disablement*, Macmillan, Basingstoke.

Packman, J. and Jordan, B. (1991) 'The Children Act: looking forward, looking back', *British Journal of Social Work*, Vol. 21 No. 4.

Pahl, J. (1985) *Private Violence and Public Policy*, Routledge & Kegan Paul, London.

Pahl, J. (1989) *Money and Marriage*, Macmillan, Basingstoke.

Papadakis, E. and Taylor-Gooby, P. (1987) *The Private Provision of Public Welfare*, Wheatsheaf, Brighton.

Parker, G. (1990) *With Due Care and Attention: a Review of Research on Informal Care*, second edition, Family Policy Studies Centre, London.

Parker, G. (1991) 'They've got their own lives to lead: carers and dependent people talking about family and neighbourhood help', in Hutton, J. *et al* (eds.) *Dependency to Enterprise*, Routledge, London.

Parker, G. (1993) *With This Body. Caring and Disability in Marriage*, Open University Press, Buckingham.

Parker, H. *et al* (1989) *Unmasking the Magistrates*, Open University Press, Buckingham.

Parker, R. (1981) 'Tending and Social Policy' in Goldberg, E. and Hatch, S. (eds.) *A New Look at the Personal Social Services*, Policy Studies Institute, London.

Parker, R. (ed.) (1991) *Looking after children: Assessing outcomes in child care*, Department of Health/HMSO, London.

Parsloe, P. (1976) 'Social Work and the Justice Model', *British Journal of Social Work*, Vol.6, No.1.

Parsons, T. (1964) *The Social System*, Routledge & Kegan Paul, London.

Parton, N. (1991) *Governing the Family: Child Care, Child Protection and the State*, Macmillan, Basingstoke.

Pascall, G. (1986) *Social Policy: a Feminist Analysis*, Tavistock, London.

Phillips, C. (1992) 'Challenging the "spectre of old age": community care for older people in the 1990s' in Manning, N. and Page, R. (eds.) *Social Policy Review 4*, Social Policy Association, Canterbury.

Piaget, J. (1932) *The Moral Judgement of the Child*, Routledge, London.

Pillsbury, B. (1978) 'Doing the month: Confinement and convalescence of Chinese Women after birth', *Social Science and Medicine*, Vol.12 pp.11- 22.

Pimentel, D. (1994) Address to the American Association for the Advancement of Science, reported in *The Guardian*, 22 February.

Pitts, J. (1986) 'Black Young People and Juvenile Crime. Some Unanswered Questions' in Matthews, R. and Young, J. (eds.) *Confronting Crime*, Sage, London.

Pitts, J. (1988) *The Politics of Juvenile Crime*, Sage, London.

Pitts, J. (1990) *Working with Young Offenders*, Macmillan, Basingstoke.

Pitts, J. (1992) 'Juvenile Justice Policy in England and Wales' in Coleman, J. and Warren-Adamson, R.C. (eds.) *Youth Policy in the 1990s*, Routledge, London.

Prestage, M. (1995) 'Tories face £200m care bill' *The Observer*, 12 March.

Pugh, G. and De'Ath, E. *Working towards partnership in the early years*, National Children's' Bureau.

Quinton, D. and Rutter, M. (1984) 'Parents with children in care', *Journal of Child Psychology and Psychiatry*, Vol. 25 No. 2.

Qureshi, H. and Walker, A. (1989) *The Caring Relationship: Elderly People and their Families*, Macmillan, London.

Rees, S. (1978) *Social Work Face to Face*, Edward Arnold, London.

Rees, S. (1991) *Achieving Power. Practice and Policy in social welfare*, Allen & Unwin, Sydney.

Rickford, F. (1993) 'Diamond Rings and Bathtime' *Social Work Today*,Vol. 25 No. 3.

Ridley, N. (1988) *The Local Right: Enabling not Providing*, Centre for Policy Studies, London.

Rimmer, L. & Wicks, M. (1983) 'The challenge of change: demographic trends, the family and social policy', in Glennerster H. (ed.) *The Future of the Welfare State*, Heinemann, London.

Roche, M. (1992) *Rethinking Citizenship: Welfare Ideology and Change in Modern Society*, Polity Press, Cambridge.

Rosenmayer, L. and Kockeis, E. (1963) 'Propositions for a Sociological Theory of Ageing and the Family', *International Social Service Journal*, Vol. 15 No. 3.

Rowe, J. and Lambert, L. (1973) *Children Who Wait*, Association of British Adoption and Fostering Agencies, London.

Rutherford, A. (1986) *Growing Out of Crime*, Penguin, Harmondsworth.

Rutter, M. and Giller, G. (1983) *Juvenile Delinquency: Trends and Perspectives*, Penguin, Harmondsworth.

Rutter, M. and Madge, N. (1976) *Cycles of Disadvantage*, Heinemann Educational, Harlow.

Salter, B. (1994) 'The Politics of Community Care: social rights and welfare limits', *Policy and Politics*, Vol. 22 No. 2.

Satyamurti, C. (1981) *Occupational Survival*, Blackwell, Oxford.

Schorr, A. (1992) *The Personal Social Services: An Outside View*, Joseph Rowntree Foundation, York.

Scrivens, E. (1992) 'Choosing Choice in Social Welfare' in Manning, N. and Page, R. (eds.) *Social Policy Review 4* , Social Policy Association, Canterbury.

Sharma, R. (1991) *The Silent Minority: Children with Disabilities in Asian Families*, National Childrens Bureau, London.

Sinclair, I. and Brown,J. (1991) 'Residential Care after Wagner' in Carter, P. *et al* (eds.) *Social Work and Social Welfare Yearbook* , Open University Press, Buckingham.

Slipman, S. and Monk, S. (1991) *Making Maintenance Pay: a Practical Scheme for Improving and Enorcing Child Maintenance*, National Council for One Parent Families, London.

Smith, G. (1980) *Social Need. Policy, practice and research*, Routledge & Kegan Paul, London.

Smith, G. and Harris, R. (1972) 'Ideologies of Need and the Organisation of Social Work Departments', *British Journal of Social Work*, Vol. 2 No. 1.

Social Security Committee (SSC) (1991a) *Second Report - Changes in Maintenance Arrangements*, Session 1990-91, HMSO, London.

Social Security Committee (SSC) (1991b) *Third Report - Changes in Maintenance: The White Paper 'Children Come First' and the Child Support Bill*, Session 1990-91, HMSO, London

Social Security Committee (SSC) (1993) *First Report - The Operation of the Child Support Act: Together with the Proceedings of the Committee relating to the Report and Minutes of Evidence*, Session 1993-94, HMSO, London.

Social Security Committee (SSC) (1994) *Fifth Report - The Operation of the Child Support Act: Proposals for Change*, Session 1993-94, HMSO, London.

Social Services Inspectorate (SSI) (1991) *Care Management and Assessment: Practitioners' Guide*, HMSO, London.

Stanworth, M. (ed.) (1987) *Reproductive Technologies: Gender, Motherhood and Medicine*, Hutchinson, London.

Stevenson, O. (1993) 'Foreword' in *Beyond blame: child abuse tragedies revisited*, Routledge, London.

Stevenson, O. and Parsloe, P. (1993) *Community Care and Empowerment,* Joseph Rowntree Foundation/Community Care, York.
Stone, N. (1977) *The Family, Sex and Marriage in England 1500-1800*, Weidenfeld & Nicolson, London.
Strong, S. (1994) 'How Is It for You?' *Community Care,* 7-13 July
Taylor, L., Lacey, R. and Bracken, D. (1980) *In Whose Best Interests? The Unjust Treatment of Children in Courts and Institutions*, Cobden Trust and MIND.
Taylor-Gooby, P. (1991) *Social Change, Social Welfare and Social Science*, Harvester Wheatsheaf, Hemel Hempstead.
Taylor-Gooby, P. (1994) 'Welfare outside the state' in Jowell, R. et al (eds.) *British Social Attitudes: the 11th report*, Dartmouth, Aldershot.
Taylor-Gooby, P. and Lawson, R. (eds.) (1993) *Markets and Managers. New Issues in the Delivery of Welfare*, Open University Press, Buckingham.
Tebbit, N. (1989) *Upwardly Mobile*, Sphere, London.
Tennstedt, S. and McKinlay, J. (1989) 'Informal care for frail older persons' in Ory, M. and Bond, L. (eds.) *Ageing and Health Care* Routledge, London.
Thatcher, M. (1981) *Welfare and the Family*, speech to WRVS, 19 January.
Thatcher, M. (1988) Interview in *Sunday Times*, 9 November.
Therborn, G. (1989) 'The Two-thirds, One-third Society' in Hall, S. and Jacques, M. (eds.) *New Times: the Changing Face of Politics in the 1990s*, Lawrence and Wishart, London.
Thiele, B. (1992) 'Vanishing Acts in Social and Political Thought: Tricks of the Trade in McDowell, L. and Pringle, R. (eds.) *Defining Women: Social Institutions and Gender Divisions*, Polity, Cambridge.
Thompson, D. (1993) 'Community Care, New Public Management and Informal Carers' unpublished, University of Luton.
Titmuss, R. (1963) *Essays on the Welfare State*, second edition, Allen & Unwin, London.
Tizard, B. (1977) *Adoption. A Second Chance*, Open Books, London.
Townsend, P. (1991) 'The Structured Dependency of the Elderly: a Creation of Social Policy in the Twentieth Century', *Ageing and Society*, Vol. 1 No. 1.
Toynbee, P. (1994) 'Family Fortunes', *The Guardian*, 2 February.
Travis, A. (1995) 'Child priorities which UK fails to meet', *The Guardian*, 28 January.

Twigg, J. (1989) 'Models of Carers: How do social care agencies conceptualise their relationship with informal carers?', *Journal of Social Policy*, Vol. 18 No. 1.

Twigg, J. and Atkin, K. (1994) *Carers Perceived. Policy and practice in informal care*, Open University Press, Buckingham.

Ungerson, C. (1981) 'Women and Caring: Skills, Tasks and Taboos', in GarmarnikowE. ,Morgan D. , PurvisJ. , and Taylorson D. (eds.) *The Public and the Private*, Heinemann, London.

Ungerson, C. (1983) 'Why do women care?', in Finch, J. and Groves, D. (eds.) *A Labour of Love*, Routledge and Kegan Paul, London.

Ungerson, C. (1987) *Policy is Personal: Sex, Gender and Informal Care*, Tavistock, London.

Utting, D. (1995) *Family and parenthood: supporting families, preventing breakdown (A guide to the debate)*, Joseph Rowntree Foundation, York.

Walker, A. (1980) 'The Social Creation of Poverty and Dependency in Old Age', *Journal of Social Policy*, Vol. 9 No. 1.

Walker, A. (1982) 'Dependency and Old Age' *Social Policy and Administration*, Vol.16 No.2.

Walker, A. (1987) 'The social construction of dependency in old age' in Loney, M. *et al* (eds.) *The State or the Market?*, Sage, London.

Walker, A. (1991) 'The social construction of dependency in old age' in Loney, M. *et al* (eds.) *The State or the Market?*, second edition, Sage, London.

Warnes, A. (1992) 'Being Old, Old People and the Burdens of Burden', *Ageing and Society*, Vol. 13 pp. 297-338.

Warnock (1984) *Report of the Committee of Inquiry into Human Fertilisation and Embryology*, HMSO, London.

Webb, A. and Wistow, G. (1987) *Social Work, Social Care and Social Planning: The Personal Social Services since Seebohm*, Longman, Harlow.

West, D. (1982) *Delinquency: its roots, careers and prospects*, Duckworth Press, London.

Wicks, M. (1991) 'Family Matters and Public Policy' in Loney, M. *et al* (eds.) *The State or the Market?*, second edition, Sage, London.

Williams, F. (1989) *Social Policy: A Critical Introduction. Issues of Race, Gender and Class,* Polity, Cambridge.

Wilson, E. (1982) 'Women, the "Community" and the "Family" in Walker, A. (ed.) *Community Care, the Family, the State and Social Policy*, Basil Blackwell/Martin Robertson, Oxford.

Wilson, G. (1993) 'Money and Independence in Old Age', in Arber, S. and Evandrou, M. (eds.) *Ageing, Independence and the Life Course*, Jessica Kingsley,
Wingham, G. (1994) 'A Child's Right', *Community Care*, 30 June.
Winnicott, D. (1965) *The maturational processes and the facilitative environment,* International Universities Press, New York.
Wistow, G. (1985) 'Community Care for the Mentally Handicapped: disappointing progress' in Harrison, A. and Gretton, J. (eds.) *Health Care UK*, Policy Journals, Hermitage.
Wistow, G., Knapp, M., Hardy, B. and Allen, C. (1994) *Social Care in a Mixed Economy*, Open University Press, Buckingham.
Young, A. (1983) 'Externalising and internalising medical belief systems: An Ethiopian example', *Social Science and Medicine*, Vol. 10 No. 3-4.

Name index

Subject index